How to Get Along with Your Pastor

How to
Get Along
with Your Pastor

Creating Partnership for Doing Ministry

George B. Thompson Jr.

THE PILGRIM PRESS

CLEVELAND

The Pilgrim Press, 700 Prospect Avenue, Cleveland, OH 44115,
thepilgrimpress.com
© 2006 by George B. Thompson Jr.

Contacting the author: George B. Thompson Jr. is associate professor of
Church Administration and Leadership at the Interdenominational
Theological Center, Atlanta. He provides training and coaching for congregations, church boards, judicatory committees, and any group seeking to
strengthen the mission of the local church and willing to learn new resources in achieving that goal.

For more information, visit www.dynamiclead.org.

Scripture quotations, unless otherwise noted, are from the New Revised
Standard Version of the Bible, © 1989 by the Division of Christian Education
of the National Council of Churches of Christ in the United States of America
and are used by permission. Changes have been made for inclusivity.

Printed in the United States of America on acid-free paper

10   09   08   07   06   5   4   3   2   1

Library of Congress Cataloging-in-Publication Data

Thompson, George B. (George Button), 1951–
    How to get along with your pastor : creating partnership for doing
  ministry / George B. Thompson, Jr.
        p. cm.
    Includes bibliographical references.
    ISBN-13: 978-0-8298-1713-3
    1. Pastoral theology.   I. Title.
BV4011.3.T47   2006
253—dc22   2006023598

ISBN-13: 978-0-8298-1713-3
ISBN-10: 0-8298-1713-1

CONTENTS

❖

INTRODUCTION

A Case for "Getting Along" with Your Pastor

I n my work as a seminary teacher, I hear stories, lots of stories. Far too many of them are about what happens between a church and its pastor when things go wrong. Some of these stories leave me trying to imagine how the congregation in question ever could recover its calling as God's people. I also wonder what happened to the pastor, when the mess is all over. Most of all, such troubling narratives leave me wondering what it takes for pastors and churches to develop the kind of rapport that creates and sustains fruitful gospel ministry.

Let me tell you one such story.

WHAT HAPPENED?

The new pastor had come with high hopes. The church had been losing members for thirty years, yet the building was located in one of the most prestigious neighborhoods in town. The search committee spoke of reaching out into the community. Rev. Morgan was up to the challenge. After some years in business, he had graduated from seminary and served a couple of other respectable congregations. Affable and organized, Rev. Morgan was well-liked in the previous congregations. He threw himself into his new ministry—with the staff, on the governing board, ministering to families in crisis, leading worship, and preaching.

Yet, in spite of all his efforts, Rev. Morgan felt like he kept running into resistance. Most board members would appear to support his ideas, until certain others voiced their displeasure. When pressed on issues, board members said little, even when church members wrote letters or appeared in the pastor's office to complain. The church budget was stretched thin, even though the music department was fully funded. Then a new staff person became demanding and uncooperative. Through it all, Rev. Morgan worked hard to keep his composure, encouraging people to talk over the issues.

In Rev. Morgan's fourth year, he began to notice that the members who had disagreed with him the most had stopped talking to him. These included Joyce, who had served on the search committee and had been the one to call and offer Rev. Morgan the position. He was so intent on working through the church's daily demands, however, that Rev. Morgan did not think much about Joyce's and the others' silence. Looking back on the situation, he wishes that he could have known what to do.

At a board meeting one night, without any warning, Joyce angrily asked Rev. Morgan to resign. He was stunned. Joyce went on to say that she spoke for "other members of the congregation." Rev. Morgan asked Joyce to name the others but she refused to do so. The other board members looked shocked. Rev. Morgan suggested that a special meeting be called to discuss the matter carefully. The board agreed. Joyce left the room silently and, a few minutes later, Rev. Morgan saw her in the church parking lot. She was sitting in a car with Ron, another board member who had just left the same meeting.

The special board meeting only seemed to make matters worse. Joyce presented "their" list of complaints, to which Rev. Morgan responded. A few of the other board members spoke of how much they appreciated Rev. Morgan's ministry, but none of them addressed Joyce. She repeated her resignation demand, "on behalf of unnamed members of the congregation." Rev. Morgan said that he needed time to think, and the meeting concluded.

Rev. Morgan did not know what to do. Shocked, angry, confused, frustrated, losing confidence daily, the conscientious pastor sought the help of denominational officers. Their responses left him feeling on his own. Nothing made sense. The church had acquired new members, renovated rooms, involved teenagers. What was going on?

At the next church board meeting, Rev. Morgan offered his resignation. In spite of his deep anger and hurt, he did not want to do anything that would cause further trouble. He said that he still did not understand what had led "the unnamed members" to be so dissatisfied with him. Morgan then stated, as calmly as he could, that the silence of the board itself was a big factor in his decision: if the board could not speak clearly to the matter, then he could not continue as their pastor. He then made two requests. One was that they work out a reasonable severance arrangement. The other was that the church board help the congregation work on its own issues, rather than supposing that everything in the church would be fine once he left.

A year after Rev. Morgan's departure, the congregation was busy looking for its next pastor. The budget had to be tightened, even though the church was paying less in salaries. Yet, in spite of Rev. Morgan's parting request, the church board had not talked at all about what had happened. On some Sundays, you could have walked through the sanctuary and overheard one of the newer church members commenting about Rev. Morgan's departure. "I still don't understand what happened. I liked Rev. Morgan; he was a good pastor, and I know other church members who feel the same way. How come nobody in the church knows anything?"

AFTERMATH

If reading this story leaves you feeling uncomfortable, or angry, or nervous, or puzzled, then perhaps your church has experienced travail of its own. Truth be told, churches go through struggles, hard time, disagreements. In spite of New Testament admonitions to "love one another," to "bear one another's burdens," to live in "holiness and godliness," our churches are not perfect.

The story of a waning church whose pastor left under a cloud is not merely the story of Rev. Morgan. Change the details here and there, and you are describing something that happens every month—yes, every month—in American churches. It has happened to me, in one of my pastoral calls. I had come to a church with every intention of getting along and doing ministry; I departed angry and feeling like a failure. The conflict was left unresolved. I became just one of hundreds of pastors joining the dubious ranks of clergy who "must have done something wrong," who couldn't hack it in the parish.

This is not a book about my pastoral story or about church conflict. You can find plenty of books written about conflict, and some of them might help your church.[1] Instead, this book tries to help church members step back and see the bigger picture. An effective pastoral relationship is more like a couple who loves to dance together or a band that plays wonderful music. If we spend too much time on the details, without remembering that we want to dance and sing, our church will not have much to offer to gospel ministry.

GETTING THINGS CLEAR

This book, then, seeks to blaze a new trail for churches who want to thrive in authentic, faithful ministry with their pastor. It is a book for church deacons, elders, and other officers who recognize that a healthy, trusting, respectful relationship between pastor and congregation becomes the foundation for the church's vitality. It is a book designed to give you the tools you need to help your pastor become the best pastor that she or he can be with you.

Having stated this purpose in positive terms, I want to say also what the book does not do:

- *It does not reinforce the church's "business as usual."* If your church has experienced a pastoral relationship that was difficult, this book does not pat you on the back, tell you to forget the pain, and allow you to carry on as you have done so in the past.

- *It does not give you permission to point fingers.* Fault-finding is a common human tendency, but it does not seem to be a very productive exercise for the church. Blaming tends to oversimplify the situation, creating an atmosphere of "us" versus "them." What is more useful in the long run is to foster an attitude of being responsible and accountable, without the tenor of a witch hunt.

◆ *It will not provide quick and easy answers.* Television commercials suggest that your need (being hungry or thirsty, getting around, trying to lose weight or look attractive) can be fulfilled simply by using the advertised product or service. American society has become oriented to the "instant fix," and churches are just as susceptible as anyone to this tendency. By contrast, strong pastoral relationships, and strong churches, take time to develop and to yield results for faith and ministry.

◆ *It is not magic.* Some churches get desperate and begin looking for fairy dust. They hope that just the right incantation—placing greeters at the right places, playing certain music in worship, or praying a certain kind of prayer—will take care of everything. Magic, however, is a poor substitute for faith, especially for God's chosen leaders (see 1 Sam. 28:3–19).

This book tries to look ahead and be honest. It rests upon several convictions that are based upon my years as a pastor and teacher. These claims interconnect and look something like this:

◆ *The twenty-first century will not be kind to congregations that are in a holding pattern.* Today's world is changing radically in many ways. Simply doing what is familiar and comfortable is like slowly drawing a sharp knife blade across your neck.

◆ *Congregations today cannot afford long to ignore their own role in pastoral relationships that do not work well.* I remember as a child my grandmother saying, "It takes two to tango!" Instead of simply blaming the pastor, a wise church examines itself, to see what it can learn about itself.

◆ *Congregations who want to do more than maintain themselves must nurture their pastoral relationships.* Want to stop treading water, to get out of being stuck? Start by learning to respect and trust each other, including your pastor.

- *Congregations can be very deliberate about what they contribute to their pastor's accomplishments with them.* Beyond a place to study and a living salary, congregations often assume that everything else depends upon the pastor. To me, this dangerous assumption grows out of the congregation's lack of self-awareness.

- *Pastors want their congregations to be authentic, faithful, and strong.* Most pastors respond to their call out of a sense of wanting to help the people of God. Pastors in touch with their vocation find their deepest satisfaction in seeing the community of faith bear strong witness to that faith.

- *Congregations (and their pastors) need to use new models of self-understanding and practice.* I have made this case elsewhere, for pastors and those who study the church. For our purposes here, I am appealing to your interest in the strength of your congregation. If the current models were adequate, we would not have so many struggling churches and denominations.

DEFAULT DRIVE

I am alerting you right now: this book ain't what you think! It addresses church concerns that are very common, yes, but its way of treating these concerns is unique. Herein you will be introduced to what I call a "culture model" for understanding churches. This model needs to be clearly identified, since its use with churches is new.

For years, our most common way of looking at our churches has been in terms of a modern business organization. Even though most pastors protest that "the church is different!" we still tend to organize our churches following business practices. Committees, meetings, votes, reports, strategic plans, job descriptions, and the like cannot be ends in themselves. Instinctively, many churches seem to know this. They are the kind of churches that are ready to learn a new model.

In recent years, pastors have been thinking about their churches with a different model. It is known as "family systems theory," and its famous proponent is Edwin Friedman.[2] Family systems lays out a set of concepts that was developed originally to help explain what happens when mom, dad, and the kids are not getting along. Its goal is to equip people who live or work with each other to develop a "healthy" rather than "dysfunctional" system or relationships.

One of the positive features of this theory is its conviction that human experience is interrelated and holistic. That is, we are always part of a network of relationships that is greater than the parts (the individual persons) by themselves. Family systems theory reminds us that we are made to be in community.

SEEING THINGS DIFFERENTLY

The culture theory model in this book is both similar to, and different from, family systems. It is similar in that it introduces a theory, one that must be learned deliberately, because it is not familiar. Culture theory also assumes that human life is holistic and interrelated. What makes culture theory different from family systems is that it is based upon anthropology, an academic discipline created to help researchers understand human communities. Rather than approaching churches simply as families, culture theory treats them like the complex, culture-creating, and culture-bearing groups that they are. In my experience as a pastor and teacher, I have found culture theory more beneficial for churches. First it helps them get a more thorough grasp on what is happening. Then it helps them figure out what decisions and actions will more clearly serve their purposes.

Although conflict is the most common reason that churches seek help, this book is not about church conflict per se. We will look at conflict in a different way since it is one of the several basic issues that pastors and congregations must negotiate. A culture model of church helps us move constructively from the realization that conflict is a symptom, not a disease, and especially that it is not necessarily a "problem." The Bible itself is full of stories of trouble among God's people, all the way from the Red Sea to Paul's fledgling churches in Asia Minor. We can approach conflict by reframing it culturally. We begin to tap into the deeper energy that makes the congregation what it is. We will then discover that this deeper energy often has very little to do with our religion!

In other words, a cultural approach to church shows us that "conflict" is normal. The most important thing about any issue where a difference of opinion is present is not that it is happening. The key to conflict resolution is in how it is handled. We cannot change our harmful patterns in conflict unless we first change our point of view. This cultural approach to church is a shift in thinking that will take time and deliberate effort to learn and use well. Yet, if you are convinced that getting along with your pastor is crucial to your church's faith and vitality, you are ready.

Our attention in this book, therefore, will be upon the congregation itself. Its cultural dynamics play a big role in the work of its pastor. The opposite is also true: the pastor's own cultural baggage affects the congregation. Pastors need to learn how to get along with their church. So I wrote that book first, for them. Now it is time for the same kind of book for you, the congregation.

LEARNING AND APPLYING

What you will find in this book, therefore, is an integration of theory with practice. This culture model is too new and too comprehensive to try to use it without first being clear about what it looks like. Part 1 of the book, then, lays out the culture theory. For some readers, this will be the hard work! Over the years, I have discovered that any group's culture can be measured in three distinct but complementary ways. For one thing, culture is *deep*—it goes below the surface of what is obvious. We usually pay so much attention to the obvious things that we miss their connections to what truly matters—down in the mud of our cultural swamp.

For another thing, culture also is *long*—it exists and changes over time. For instance, long-time members of a well-established church tend to lose touch with the energy that drove the congregation in its earliest years. Being aware of what usually changes in culture over time gives churches tools for maintaining their vitality. Finally, culture is *wide*—it occurs across a vast scale. One end of this scale is as small as the "subculture" of a women's church auxiliary; the other end is as large as the "macroculture" of the United States. These terms are among a number of words that we will define in specific ways.

Some of the other terms that you will learn and use in this book are:

Submerged beliefs—deeply held assumptions the congregation rarely thinks about or discusses but that govern everything that they consider true, acceptable, and right

Dominant subculture—that segment of the congregation's life and practices that has more influence than any other segment

Cultural capital—invisible but powerful assets and resources valued by and exchanged within the congregation, based in its own cultural "swamp" (see chapter 1)

Key culture bearers—persons who have gained sufficient cultural capital to be recognized as standing for the well-being of the congregation and speaking for what it most treasures

Lifecycle—a series of predictable phases faced by every congregation as it goes through the years facing opportunities and solving problems

Decline—the inability and/or unwillingness of the congregation to respond to change that occurs around it (a cultural phenomenon, not a numerical value)

Mesoculture—one of several "streams of culture" (see chapter 3) that exist, flowing in between the local community around a church and the large-scale American society, with its own culture

With this cultural framework developed in part 1, we then will move in part 2 to application. We will consider several topics that cover a pastor's tenure with a particular congregation. These include the all-important questions of pastoral "adoption" by the congregation, as well as of power, leadership, conflict, and change. Determining what these topics look like through the culture lens is our initial task, as we then see how strategies could look different because we are thinking culturally. All along, the vantage point is the congregation itself, especially how the cultural lens helps your congregation figure out its role with the pastor in doing ministry.

In preparation for the upcoming discussion, consider, then, these questions, addressed to your congregation as a whole:

- Before your pastor arrives, how can you become a self-aware, hospitable host to this stranger who joins your community?
- How does your church's power reveal itself? Who has it, and why?
- Is your church able to change, or is it stuck in the mud?
- How are decisions made? Do you work together, really?
- Can you take good risks? Does your "walk" match your "talk"?

Part One

"KNOW THYSELF"

A Cultural Approach to Congregational
Self-Understanding and Honesty

In this first part of the book, you will read introductions to the framework that we will use throughout. Getting along with your pastor is a more intricate venture than simply whether or not you like the person. The following three chapters lay the groundwork for why this is the case. Many of the potential difficulties between you and your pastor can be understood better by seeing them culturally. You will learn how to see your church's culture—by digging deeply, by looking across time, and by paying attention to what is outside your immediate circumstances. Each one of these chapters includes diagrams to help you learn how the models work.

Pay particular attention to the terminology used. Become familiar with what each one of the terms means, with how it is used here, rather than with what you think it means in another context. Be sure to spend time with the questions at the end of each chapter. Make them a topic of thoughtful discussion among other church members. They will help you apply each culture model to your own congregation. Then you will benefit more from the discussion in part 2.

❖ *one* ❖

CULTURAL DEPTHS

Your Church's Swamp

"CHURCH" IS LIKE . . .

When you think of "church," what images come to mind?

For instance, what if you thought of your church as a pillar?[1] A pillar is a massive post or column used to hold up a section of a building. Many ancient Greek temples and buildings eventually crumbled, but many of their columns stand to this day. Some churches are like that: they exist over the years, even when worn, and stand out in their communities.

We also could think about church as a pilgrim. We remember the Pilgrims out of England, whose early years in North America were eased by the generosity of tribes who already lived here. Pilgrim churches became a "home away from home in their new home," places to affirm cultural identity and values, to make the best of traditions.

Still other congregations might be best described as survivors. At one time, the towns where these churches are located thrived, providing schools, jobs, homes, and social opportunities. Yet things change, and neighborhoods can go from strong to distressed quickly as economic conditions decline. These churches now do not have many resources, but they do their best in a changing community.

A few churches could be called prophets. Inspired by biblical voices like those of Jeremiah and Amos, prophet churches speak and act in the public square. They are not afraid to take an unpopular position on a social issue, if members believe that they are being faithful to God. Prophet churches often are not very big, and they expect a lot from their members.

One of the more popular images of church seems to be that of servant. Jesus urged his followers to be "slave of all" (Mark 10:44) and Paul admonished believers to "bear one another's burdens, and in this way you will fulfill the law of Christ" (Gal. 6:2). Many long-established churches in small towns exemplify the low-key, giving ways of the servant, where people know each other and help out when someone is down.

Pillar; pilgrim; survivor; prophet; servant. Each one of these images captures something of the rich life of congregations. None of them tries to tell the whole story. *Which image sounds the most like your church?*

"CHURCH" IS LIKE WHAT?!

Let's try one more image, although I doubt that this one has crossed your mind. Let's imagine your church as a swamp! A swamp does not sound very appealing, does it? Murky, tangled, dangerous to outsiders—these are pictures that don't fit our ideals for our churches. We know our church is not perfect, but still—a swamp?

The swamp image of church can be useful, because it works no matter what other image of your church you wish to employ. This is because we can use "swamp" as a metaphor to understand your church's *culture*. As I often say to students and pastors, churches create, nurture, and transmit culture. In this regard, they are like any other group that human beings put together. To speak of your church as a swamp means that we are paying attention to its culture.

There are a couple of other reasons why the image of church as a swamp is helpful. For one thing, swamps appear to be quite stable, even though they can and do change over time, based on climatic conditions and outside influences. The same is true for the culture of your church. It does not change quickly and certainly not easily—but it can and will change, even as it retains some of its cherished characteristics.

Another reason to use the swamp metaphor might be the most important one of all. The cultural swamp explains elements of your church's life that are often missed, that are hard to pinpoint, but that make all the difference nonetheless. These deeper elements almost dictate whether or not your church will get along with its pastor.

THE POWER OF THE SWAMP

Our task in this chapter, then, is to take our first look at how culture functions. As I wrote in the introduction, *we can observe culture operating in three distinctive, yet overlapping, ways.* One way is to look at culture's depths. The image of a swamp presents us with a tongue-in-cheek yet revealing set of tools for examining our church. A swamp is beautiful in its own way, a complex part of God's world, as an environment that has to do its own balancing and changing over time. Even its snakes and alligators can contribute to our appreciation of what a swamp reveals about our church.

WADING INTO THE SWAMP

When we examine a swamp, we notice that it consists of three very basic parts. If we only glance quickly at the swamp, we might conclude that it has only two layers—the shore and the water. It is easy to overlook the third layer, the deeper layer beneath. Our attention can be diverted easily to all the activity and elements on top—plants, bushes, vines, various species of trees, animals of all sizes and shapes, insects, and so on. This part of the swamp is easy to notice; we will name it the *stuff*, because there is a whole bunch of it. Swamp stuff, like church stuff, tends to get our attention readily. It can be beautiful, interesting, complicated, boring, threatening, confusing, and more. The stuff is on the shore of the swamp, where most of the action appears to be.

In our churches, the stuff on the cultural shore of the swamp also appears to be where most of the action is. Think about all the observable stuff in your congregation:

- worship services
- Sunday school and education programs
- fellowship activities
- outreach ministries
- sanctuary, fellowship hall, kitchen, classrooms, parlor, and other facilities of the physical plant
- members, visitors, friends, and so on

To a visitor, new member, or new pastor, all of this stuff can seem overwhelming, even when it appears familiar.

If you try to explain to a church visitor what your church's stuff stands for, you would be moving to the swamp's next layer. This layer consists of *sayings* that float *in the water*, representing the values and purposes that your church puts forth. These values and purposes express your church at its best, its most fully hoped-for ideals:

- "The pastor's casual dress lets visitors know that they can come as they are."
- "We open with praise music to remind ourselves that God is always worthy of our praise."
- "We built a gymnasium because our kids and the neighborhood kids need a place to play that is safe and welcomes them."
- "We encourage small groups because our members need to grow in their faith by developing friendships and spiritual support inside our large congregation."
- "Speaking in tongues is a sign that the power of the Holy Spirit is present in our midst."

Sometimes our church's sayings end up in slogans like "We are a warm and friendly church," "Here there are no big 'I's or little 'U's," "A Christ-centered, Spirit-filled people," "A church for the rest of us," and so on. Sayings like these and others float in the cultural water of your congregation. They are grounded in our theologies and spiritual aspirations. Because they express meanings of importance, they sound good; they put your church in a favorable light.

Yet, are the sayings true? That is, are they able to explain everything on the cultural shore of your church? I used to think so. In my denomination, when a pastor is looking for a call to a church and a church is looking to call a pastor, both of them write up their dossiers. Supposedly, the information in the dossiers and interviews will provide both parties with a complete enough picture of each other. Based on my pastoral experience, however, this process does not work effectively. Why not?

The answer is that the cultural swamp of your church goes deeper than the stuff on the shore and the sayings in the water. In nature, water refracts light: objects in the water appear in one place but are actually located slightly off from where our eyes tell us they are. Below the surface of the water, even below the water itself, is the swamp's lowest layer, the part of the swamp that is its foundation—the mud. The mud is what supports the swamp, what holds the water, what helps give the swamp its life.

Down in the mud of our church's cultural swamp, we discover what is *submerged*. This submerged material consists of deeply held beliefs that have almost no religious character of

DIAGRAM A—Layers in a Cultural Swamp

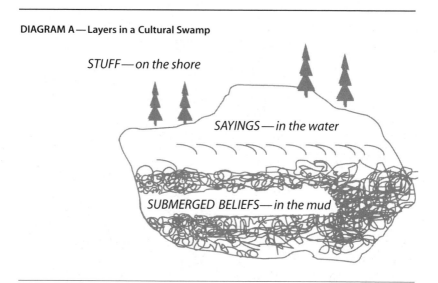

STUFF—on the shore

SAYINGS—in the water

SUBMERGED BELIEFS—in the mud

their own. Furthermore, they exist for the most part outside of the church's conscious awareness. They are assumed to be true in a nonnegotiable way. In spite of their being virtually invisible and relatively imperceptible, these submerged beliefs hold all the clues to your church's culture and thus to its life. What is submerged down in the mud, once it is uncovered and examined, reveals if your church's sayings are validated or contradicted.

So, *what do submerged beliefs look like? How did they get there? And why are they so powerful?*

SORTING THROUGH THE MUD

Submerged beliefs are perceptions based in fundamental aspects of life[2] that the congregation learned together, especially in its earlier years of formation. Any new group has to try things out to see what happens and what works. At some point a congregation learns, *through its interpretation of its experiences,* that it can trust certain deep beliefs to be self-evident to them. This kind of learning does not happen the same way that someone learns how to divide fractions or operate a computer. Cultural learning is more subtle than that, which is one reason why it needs to be taken so seriously.

Beliefs about Time

To gain a clearer grasp on this critical part of the swamp model, let us consider one example. Every congregation maintains a few submerged beliefs concerning the nature of *time*. Such beliefs usually derive from cultural sources somewhere in the society or world outside of the congregation proper. Research reveals several ways in which societies in the world treat time. Some communities (whether ethnic or organizational) are oriented toward the *past,* others toward the *present,* and still others toward the *future.* You probably have known, for instance, a congregation that had little energy for looking ahead but could revel in memories of the glorious days gone by. This would be an example of a submerged belief about time as past. Thus, *congregations can possess in their cultural mud different attitudes toward how they see themselves in time.*

Another example of divergent submerged beliefs about time has to do with how it is understood to be available. Most of the people who read this book will assume that we can divide time up into parts, one after another, and use them in a sequence. Books on time management, unionized work days and weeks, world records, standardized test-taking, and even Leap Day are all examples of this kind of time. This view of time appears, however, to be quite recent in history, concentrated in societies that derive from northern European countries.

By contrast, much of the rest of the world tends to approach time in terms of the things that get done, by opportunities of the occasion, rather than by clock measurements.

One year during college, a summer job took me to a Native American reservation for a week. While there, I became aware of the quiet and gentle ways of the native residents. One day my car would not start. I had to drive somewhere the next day, so the pastor of the church got together a couple of the other men and took a look under the hood. They worked on my car for eight hours to fix it, and without a break! I was almost frantic, knowing that I did not have enough money to pay even one mechanic for eight hours of work on my car. When the pastor refused to take any payment, I was so relieved with their generosity that I missed a lesson about time. In their tribal society, time was not divided up the way that it was for me at school and work. In their cultural world (read here, "submerged beliefs in the mud"), fixing my car took the time that it took.

This kind of confusion over different beliefs about time's "availability" not infrequently occurs in the way that Christians interpret references to time in the Bible. There are two primary words for "time" in the New Testament Greek. One is χρονος, *chronos* in our alphabet, from which words like "chronology" are derived. The meaning of *chronos* represents the understanding of time that has come to dominate modern life, that of dividing time in amounts that are carefully measured. Yet this form of time apparently is not the most common way in the New Testament world that time is understood. A sampling of references to "time" there yields a surprise: most of the Greek terms for time are not *chronos* but καιρος, or *kairos,* a word that means something distinctly different. *Kairos* would be translated more accurately by the English words "opportunity," "moment," or "occasion."[3] Many verses thus connote a different nuance about time when one translates *kairos* carefully, as in these instances:

"The *opportunity* is fulfilled and the realm of God has come near." (Mark 1:15)

"[The devil] departed from him until a *moment of opportunity.*" (Luke 4:13)

"See, now is the acceptable *occasion.*" (2 Cor. 6:2)

Americans easily tend to impose a submerged belief about time as "chronos" on their reading of the Bible. Christianity's own heritage out of the scriptures leans much more heavily on the view of time that I experienced with the generous tribal men who worked on my car. Unless we are aware of differences in the contents of the mud of one cultural swamp compared with another, we could easily draw conclusions about things that are incorrect.

Not Religious Sources

Thus, submerged beliefs in the cultural mud of any church include deep assumptions about the nature of time, as well as assumptions about how we know what is true, what is real, various aspects of being human, and so on. It is not necessary for our purposes here to discuss any of these categories in detail. It is crucial, however, to realize that these submerged beliefs do exist and that *they characteristically represent assumptions that are not particularly religious in nature.* Certainly, for instance, submerged beliefs about "truth" (all the way from "Truth comes only through direct revelation by God" to "Truth is whatever works for you") end up influencing our religious views significantly. Yet we will mislead ourselves and hamper our ability to gain adequate insight into our cultural swamps if we think that religious statements tell the whole story. They do not; they are, if you recall, part of the sayings that float in the water of your church's culture. As such, they play a role, but *only as they con-*

nect particular stuff on the shore with actual submerged beliefs in the mud.

The power of what is lodged in the mud is closely related to how it gets there. As we noted briefly above, *any organization's submerged beliefs become what they are as a result of its experiences.* In its beginning, a congregation has no history and must create its life by trying out a multitude of ideas and practices. The ways in which that congregation makes sense out of what it sees as the results of its efforts generates the production of submerged beliefs. This process is not one that a church undertakes in any self-conscious or deliberate way. It just happens—and, even more importantly, it is so deep and so foundational that the submerged beliefs cannot and do not change quickly or easily.

Think, for example, about a young church, several years old, with its founding pastor, small group of founding members and a current membership of one hundred. This congregation has strengthened its life and growth by espousing such values as "God's love can overcome anything" and "You are the next member of our family." So what will the church members think when the pastor announces one Sunday morning that Deacon Jones is no longer a member of this church? Deacon Jones had been very giving of his time and talent. Suddenly, he is gone, with no explanation. Quiet rumors begin to circulate about causes of his departure.

This anecdote helps us see some things about the origins and power of what is in your church's mud. For one thing, it helps us recognize the great challenge of the church's sayings being *consistent* with its submerged material. Jesus sometimes called the scribes and Pharisees "hypocrites" because they said one thing and did something else (Matt. 23:13–31). The swamp model of church shows us why merely being good at saying what is important to the church is not enough. All the acceptable behaviors of the congregation (stuff on the shore) exist and function as they do because there are submerged elements in its mud that support them. The question is, do the sayings connect stuff on the shore with the things in the mud? More deeply, what do the sayings leave out that an outside observer can see readily? How prepared are the pastor and key members of the congregation to examine the mud, to become aware of the degree of consistency?

Deacon Jones' story also suggests that submerged beliefs emerge not only from the congregation's experience with *accomplishment*, but also with its handling of *crisis*. When a church faces a challenge—like raising money to construct its first building—and is able to meet that challenge, it will create (which means that it is "learning" something) a submerged belief that is *positive*. That belief probably will never be spoken out loud or thought consciously in members' minds. Yet the church would be learning a submerged belief such as, "People who work together and trust each other can get many things done."

So, what happens when the challenges of a crisis become a conflict that is handled in a way that leaves the church troubled? The submerged belief that ends up in its cultural mud is likely to be more *negative*, such as "People who do not go along with the pastor have to leave the church." (Note that this submerged belief, while it refers to the congregation itself, does not have an explicit religious quality about it.) Such a belief indeed could be reflecting the lived experience of the congregation from that moment of crisis, but will it help them ten years from now? Although it can be hard work, we must learn not only to uncover what is in the mud, we must be willing as a church to be honest about which beliefs will serve us well now and in the future and which ones will not.

Contents: Helpful or Otherwise?

Every submerged belief in the mud of your church's cultural swamp is there because, at one point in time, it helped your congregation. "Helping" does not necessarily mean that the experiences leading to a submerged creation were constructive or pleasant—as the story above suggests. Sometimes survival becomes the primary factor, even when decisions are handled less than well. What becomes dangerous for your church, however, is when such beliefs indeed exist in your mud but *the circumstances out of which they were born no longer are true.* Perhaps Deacon Jones wanted the church to do something very different than its founding pastor thought best. Young churches do need to focus clearly, use their resources wisely, and avoid the temptation to try to do too much. Later in its life, we cannot say categorically that this congregation will be served well by operating under that assumption that "People who do not go along with the pastor have to leave the church." Will this work helpfully when its founding pastor has died or has left?

We have taken a fair amount of time elaborating upon the bottom layer of a church's cultural swamp. We have spent more time on it, the mud, than on the other two layers, the stuff and the sayings. This is because the swamp is defined by what is in the mud, not by the stuff and the sayings. Did you hear that? *The swamp is defined by what is in the mud,* not by anything on the shore of the church's culture or floating in its swamp water. You might think that what "makes" your church is something like its beautiful sanctuary, its preaching, the quality of the music, the emphasis on educating and mentoring youth, its commitment to improving quality of life in the neighborhood, and the like. However, unless you identify the connections between that stuff and what is in your mud, you will mislead yourself and others. From the standpoint of the swamp model, *the single greatest challenge to churches today is to learn how to pay attention to what is in their mud.* Nothing else will help in the long run, for culture runs deep and strong.

OUT OF THE SWAMP: IMPLICATIONS FOR YOUR CHURCH

What difference can it make to your church to think of itself in the terms of a swamp? Let us identify several claims that already have suggested themselves to us.

One, the swamp model of church culture draws our attention to how *churches are truly multifaceted.* They are never as straightforward as we suppose them to be. Sometime events or circumstances occur in your church that are hard to understand. Using the swamp to get at the layers, especially down into the mud, is your best bet for clarification.

This point suggests, two, that we learn to *look beyond the surface.* Particularly during episodes of congregational disagreement, it is vital to the long-term vitality of the church to realize that "the issue" is not the issue. Culture reminds us that, to an important extent, what plays out on the stage in any one scene stands for more than the details involved. Because churches are cultural in nature, they also are highly symbolic—and not necessarily in aesthetic or noble ways. This point might be as pertinent for pastor-church relationships as for anything else. Your pastor needs to be understood as functioning in a congregational *role,* the expectations of which are both clear and veiled. This means that anything the pastor does represents something about the congregation, whether it likes it or not. There is always more at stake for the church than whether someone gets what he or she wants.

Three, since there are submerged things in the mud, and nobody talks about them, it is possible for someone new like a pastor to *stir things up* by accidentally kicking one of them. I often speak of this phenomenon as "stepping on landmines." Most pastors whom I know are well-intentioned; they do not want to create a stir in the church. Yet, they do not know where the "sacred cows" are. Let's say that your church has a beautiful parlor that is under the complete control of the church's women's society. If your new pastor comes in and insists on having a key to the parlor, what will happen? Something could explode! Here is where you as church members could help head off a disaster in the making. Many of you are "enculturated" into the church's swamp. You understand that the parlor key (stuff on the shore) and its accompanying saying ("The women are in charge of everything about the parlor") are connected to something in the mud (unspoken but understood, something like: "Women play a significant but limited role in this church"). What is your responsibility to the office of pastor to help the person in that office to navigate your swamp?

Your congregation will be better off as it learns to teach its pastors about the deepest aspects of itself.

Four, the swamp provides you with a way to understand an elusive but highly potent phenomenon in every church. It is that of *cultural capital,* which refers to *the capacity for action and influence within a community or organization, based upon the idiosyncratic qualities of its ethos or way of life.* Cultural capital comes with the territory of culture: since every organization creates, nurtures, and transmits culture, every organization also generates the unspoken parameters within which capacity for action and influence can be exercised. Cultural capital is a more specialized way to speak about the power that a particular organization or community recognizes and/or allows. Church members who participate in stuff on the shore in a way that connects them to submerged beliefs in the mud possess some measure and form of that church's cultural capital.

This notion of cultural capital is central to a cultural understanding of your church. If you want your church to have a productive gospel ministry, it must find a way to allow your pastor to have access to some of its cultural capital. This task is necessary but possible only as the church's *key culture bearers* understand and permit such pastoral access. These persons usually have been members of the church for a long time, earning the respect of (or at least tacit support from) the church as a whole.

Five, acknowledging the cultural depths of your church's swamp can help you to *become aware of its sources of inconsistency.* This is especially important for older congregations, where longtime members cherish certain memories, rituals, and objects, forgetting how long it took them to become enculturated. As we will see in the next chapter, any organization that experiences a change in its context not only begins to lose its connection to that context, but the very submerged material that the congregation cherishes also begins to lose its relevance, since that original context that supported the church's growth is now disappearing. It is tempting for the church to suppose that it can survive anyway, without examining whether the connections from shore to mud are still steady and strong. Thus, the challenge to churches in this circumstance can be daunting. On the other hand, the alternative of doing nothing only ensures decline and therefore a waning capacity for gospel witness.

Sixth and last, the cultural swamp model provides you with a nonthreatening tool for the *congregation's ongoing self-discovery.* I say "nonthreatening" purposely, because I am very aware how formidable it can seem for a church to "get down in its own mud." The things that any organization takes for granted are not that easy to talk about. In my experience as a church trainer and coach, I have seen the swamp model neutralize the fear that people might have felt. More than once, I have heard participants in a day of cultural discovery say, "This is the first time that our church ever has talked about any of this material before." Once a congregation discovers that it can discover its depths with realism and grace, it is on its way to becoming a learning congregation. Then it can engage its pastor for Christian witness and leadership.

CONCLUSION: READ THE SWAMP—AND MORE

This chapter has looked at culture from the perspective of depth. Depth alone does not explain origins or the challenge of a change process. Why are cultures in newer churches easier to adapt than in older churches? Why do young churches seem to rely on their pastors more than well-established churches? In the next chapter, we will learn how culture exists and changes over time. Our image will be that of "lifecycle," representing a model that answers some of the questions that the swamp does not. So prepare to think about your congregation's life over its years of existence, whether a few or many. The lifecycle model has its own tales to reveal!

FOR REFLECTION AND ACTION

1a. *For churches that call their pastors—Think about your last call process and information form or profile that you wrote:*

- ◆ What evidence, if any, was there of what is in your church's cultural mud?
- ◆ What would your church have to do to identify submerged beliefs and assess their current value?
- ◆ How can you discuss all three levels of your cultural swamp with a pastoral candidate, honestly and hopefully?

1b. *For churches that receive appointed pastors:*

- ◆ What do you tell the presiding elder, district superintendent, and/or bishop about your congregation?

- What do you think those denominational officers say to others about you?
- How has your church been hurt during the ministry of one of its pastors? How has this experience affected the congregation?

2. *Think about the last time there was a difference of opinion in your church:*
   - What do you think might be a couple of the submerged beliefs in the mud that long-time church members felt were being threatened?
   - What would it look like for your pastor and the congregation to use the swamp model of culture to understand and work through church dissent?

3. *Consider your current pastor (or, if a vacant pulpit, your previous one):*
   - How well-accepted is she or he?
   - To what specific actions and/or statement of his or hers can you point, that would explain this degree of acceptance?
   - What deep beliefs (submerged in the mud) in the church do you think might be at stake in light of these actions or statements?
   - What can you do to help your pastor understand your church better?

4. *If it could admit it, what is your church afraid of?*
   - What can you do to help the congregation talk about it?
   - Who has the cultural capital to help the church face its fear?
   - What church "sayings" (Bible verses or stories, songs, theological affirmations) can be reaffirmed to help overcome this fear?

❖ *two* ❖

CULTURE OVER TIME

Your Church's Lifecycle

CHURCH MOUSE LISTENS IN

When members of your church get together, what do they talk about?

For some churches, members talk enthusiastically about how they are growing in their faith. They speak with appreciation about sermons, choirs, study classes, small groups, Habitat for Humanity home builds, and other ways that the congregation's various activities nurture their life in God. Even when something or someone in the church is critiqued, the tone of conversation is never disparaging or catty. Overall, members exude a sense of enriching excitement about being part of a vibrant congregation.

In other churches, when members get together, talk turns to the mechanics of church business. Members are very conscious about who has been elected or appointed to which positions, which committees or ministry teams are doing what (and what others think about it), and how well they think the pastor and other church staff are doing in their jobs. Energy in these conversations revolves around the inner workings of the congregations, with all the programs, people, and resources that are involved.

In still other churches, when members get together, the talk eventually turns nostalgic. These churches have a dwindling number of young members; the older ones joined the church decades ago and, over that long period of time, have performed every duty accessible to them. Previous pastors often become the topic of conversation, especially the one or two who were very popular in their day. Without necessarily coming right out and saying it, members in these churches tend to center conversations around remembering the "good old days" and wondering why things can't be like they used to be.

In which one of these three scenarios do you find your church's voice most clearly? When you read each scenario, how did you feel about "that kind" of church? Does one of them seem to you to be more like the way that church "ought" to be than the others? Why? Do any of them seem negative to you? On what basis? Or do you believe that all of these scenarios could characterize congregations that are faithful, strong, and resourceful in the gospel ministry?

As we think together about how your church can get along well with its pastor, these questions are not irrelevant. Those of us who have been active in congregations for many years realize that there are differences among them. As we saw in chapter 1, some of those differences are best understood in terms of the peculiar qualities of each church's own cultural swamp.

A TIMELY TOPIC

In this chapter, we will look at another way in which differences between churches can be identified. We will see how a church's culture can and does change over time, usually a period of years, and how this kind of measurement takes on a pattern that is very predictable. "Culture over time" is a description for analyzing churches, using the model of a lifecycle. In chapter 1, we sliced through culture to its depths; here we consider culture across a church's history.

Your church's current place on the lifecycle curve has a big effect on all kinds of things:

It indicates the church's relative balance between the things that it is used to doing and the opportunity to try new things. Congregations that have existed for quite a number of years tend to become very comfortable with a certain way of worshiping, executing their activities, and using their resources. Certainly, some level of familiarity and comfort is necessary to any organization's well-being. That same comfort, however, can become a barrier of resistance when a new possibility presents itself. Lifecycle theory gives churches a chance to see when their routine practices might be getting in the way of what they say they want.

It suggests how open is your church to new people—not simply to have new members, but to including others in the center of the church's life. If I had a dollar for every church member of every church who has said to me, "We want to attract new members," I could retire to Tahiti! As we saw in chapter 1, statements like this one fall into the cultural swamp category that we have named "sayings." Sayings represent our churches' conscious aspirations, those things that members believe out loud are important to them. The key issue, however, is whether those same sayings are supported by what is in the mud, those deeply submerged attitudes and views that actually govern your church's life. *Lifecycle theory can help churches understand the extent to which they mean what they say.* In particular, lifecycle theory points out where churches will struggle to involve new members or welcome visitors as fully as their intentions might indicate.

It points out what kind of basic tasks your pastor must be able to accomplish with you. Sometimes in class I ask students to name a pastor of some well-known megachurch in the area. Then I ask them how effective they think that pastor would be if she or he suddenly became pastor of a small, ninety-year-old church in a neighborhood that had been abandoned by businesses, residents with many resources, and the interest of city government. What leads us to suppose that a megachurch and a struggling church need the same things from their pastors? Students get the point quickly: the kinds of challenges that face a new pastor are affected directly by the church's location on the lifecycle. It is critical for your church to look beyond what it says it wants and be honest about what it needs first. Otherwise, you are setting up your new pastor for failure—and you end up blaming the pastor, not yourself, for the failure of ministry.

For these three reasons and more, your church will benefit by its officers and key members becoming adept at appraising where you are on the cycle. Without a tool like this lifecycle model, your church faces years of floundering and frustration; that I can pretty much guarantee! Your pastor wants you to succeed in ministry. Let's find out how lifecycle can help blessings flow.

A BIT OF BACKGROUND

As you might expect, lifecycle theory was not developed originally to talk about churches. Rather, its earliest theoretical discussions can be found in the literature of business management. Over the years, I have met with many pastors who resist the idea that a model from business can be useful in church. "The church is different!" they have often told me. Perhaps this reticence is not as widespread among lay members as with their clergy. Many models that have been designed to help us understand various kinds of group behavior can be easily adapted and readily applied to churches. This practice of adaptation began some years ago. For instance, the church management course that I took in seminary in the 1970s used a business management textbook. The professor's lectures laid out many points from various theories of organization.

Organizational theory is one example of adapting "worldly" resources to religious purposes. Organizational theory has become a serious academic discipline, one that can be traced to the turn of the twentieth century, and one that continues to develop.[1]

Lifecycle: An "Open System"

The specific school of thought out of which this lifecycle theory arises is a cluster of theories commonly known as "open system." An open system theory begins with the claim that every organization functions integrally related to its particular context. In other words, the central factor in an open system theory is *the relationship between the organization and its environment* (the world around it). If that environment—that context, whether it be a town, a city neighborhood, or a rural region—is young and growing, its churches tend to be the same. If that environment is well-established and stable, so are most of its churches. If that environment is struggling to survive, the churches there tend to reflect that same struggle. *An open system perspective on congregations begins with the unshakeable connections between a church and its community.*

Open system theory also *defines its understanding of "growth" and "decline" differently.* In an open system model, measurable, numerical elements (for example, worship attendance, membership, budget, etc.) are not ignored; they just are not viewed as the final word. What is more important is responsiveness to context. Growth and decline are functions of the organization's willingness and ability to respond to change that is taking place around it. Churches that behave as though they can continue doing what they have always done are declining already.

This shift of definitions forces us to look at numerical changes in our churches in a different way. For instance, numerical growth in a church's early years does suggest responsiveness to its context: the congregation is taking advantage of available opportunities. By contrast, churches that are "holding their own" in terms of membership, program, and budget have usually begun to decline. Keeping worship attendance steady while your neighborhood is drastically changing usually means that your church is not changing, just doing the same things harder. *Open system theory offers any organization, especially a church, a clear way to keep the deeper questions before it.* "How do changes in the world around us affect our pursuit of our stated purpose for existing?"

These open system characteristics of "organization/environment" and "growth/decline" set the stage for our introduction to the church in lifecycle.

LIFECYCLE THEORY: FOUNDATIONS

People who write to help congregations have referred to lifecycle theory for a number of years. However, as a tool for churches, it has not been developed clearly or applied widely. To appreciate how much lifecycle can reveal about your church, we will familiarize ourselves with two sets of concepts upon which the theory is built.

A Necessary Tension

Organizations need to be able to use any and all of their resources for stated goals in such a way that they do not run out of those resources before the goal is met. The same is true for churches: if there is no place to meet and no one knows when to worship, what then? For these reasons, it is necessary for a church to become self-controlled, to manage itself.

At the same time, *organizations need to learn how to be flexible*. Declining organizations do not attend to the characteristics around them that are not the way that they used to be. When it becomes too self-managed, an organization gets stuck in a rut, repeating what is familiar and preferred. Its comfortable patterns, as successful as they might have been at one time, do not serve the organization well. At that point, it needs to learn how to be flexible again, for the capacity to modify its goals and activities was the hallmark of that organization in its early days.

In other words, the need to *modify* and the need to *self-manage* are both necessary. These two traits are *two ends of a necessary continuum*. It is never a matter of strengthening one and eliminating the other. Churches that get along well with their pastor have learned the challenge of balancing these two traits. "Balancing" does not mean neutralizing but rather living with the necessary tension in a creative way.

Four Things Your Church Cannot Do Without

Lifecycle theory also is built upon the essential interactions that create the movement of the lifecycle itself. These essential interactions occur between four primary functions that are features of every organization, including churches. These four functions apply to the church regardless of its size, age, denomination, theology, or complexity. We will designate these four functions with the terms "perform," "relate," "execute" and "envision."

"Perform" is the organization's "what" function, which has to do with all the activities in which the organization engages as a result of its purpose. Like businesses, governments, and other organizations, churches do things, too. Their activities can usually be distinguished in about five categories:

- *Worship*—faith-filled gatherings to praise God, hear the Word and celebrate sacraments and ordinances

- *Fellowship*—fostering relationships among the members, so that the congregation bonds together
- *Nurture*—support and care for the church's members, in times of need, struggle, and transition
- *Education*—learning experiences that increase members' knowledge of the common faith, spiritual development, and capacity for faithful witness
- *Outreach and service*—engaging both short-term and long-term community needs

At various times in a church's life, one or another of these categories of "performance" will command the congregation's attention. What is most important here is to recognize that churches, like other organizations, do things; they perform something.

"Execute" is the organization's "how" function, for taking care of the business of being in business. In other words, every organization has to figure out ways to support all of its activity with structures, processes, and use of resources. In traditional language, this function is called "administration." This term, however, might mislead us, especially as we think about this function as churches engage it. Not all "executing" functions are the formal ones that involve hierarchy, job descriptions, meetings, evaluation, and the like. The execute function also can and does include the informal processes, practices that emerge over time because of the particular people and specific circumstances involved.

For instance, I was pastor of a small church once where all the long-time members knew which one of them would do which tasks around the building. The congregation's board of trustees had the official responsibility for all facilities (formal). Its actual mode of operating, however, was dominated by hearing reports from longtime church board members about their activities around the building during the previous month. Any decisions about budget expenditures had been made ahead of time, by casual conversations after Sunday worship (informal). Both formal and informal approaches to the "execute" function can be useful and, indeed, in many organizations the two combine for the greatest efficiency.

"Relate" is the organization's "who" function, and it might be the most elusive one to clarify. This is because "who" refers not only to all the various constituencies of people who are associated with the organization, but also to the sense of being connected that the organization engenders. It is more difficult to pinpoint the *esprit de corps,* the affinity, the feeling of belonging that your group fosters and supports among all of its constituents. The ideal is to avoid either possible extreme. Too much affinity creates strong cliques that look out for each other more than for the well-being of the group overall. Too little affinity weakens the group's atmosphere of trust and respect, which undergird its ability to make good decisions and work together. Yet this "relating" function holds the key to creating organizations that can manage all of the lifecycle challenges most productively.

Understandably, the "relate" function is of special relevance to churches. After all, many churches speak readily about being like a family, about loving as God loves us and showing compassion for each other. There is something about Christian faith, and many other religions, for that matter, that calls forth the better side of human nature. We are convinced that people of faith should cooperate in developing a group identity that transcends what we would experience otherwise.

In its strict meaning, however, relatedness has more to do with what actually happens. What behaviors does the organization exhibit that provide clues to ways in which people connect and participate with each other? Churches can be as excluding as anyone else and rarely are as welcoming as they say they are.

"Envision" is the "why," the final organizational function that we will introduce here, but that is not because it is of low priority. Rather, "envision," like "relate," is significant in part because it is somewhat elusive. While "perform" and "execute" are concrete functions, directly measurable, "relate" and "envision" are more qualitative. These latter two emphasize properties that one feels more than sees. In the case of "envision," what one feels is the sense of direction, the purpose that the organization is following. Purpose here has to do with a *vision of the future,* imagined in a picture of the way that things could be that

has not been fully realized. This description of envisioning as an organizational function holds true for any organization.

For churches, the "envision" function plays the same formal role as in any other organization. Of course, what makes this function distinctive for churches is the potential for a distinctive content to vision. Hopefully, churches stand up for the highest ideals of faith, life together, and a society that more fully realizes God's purposes for creation. Keeping a vision clear and strong is an ongoing organizational task, for churches as much as for any other group. Many churches today, tragically, have allowed their visions almost to flicker out. When this happens, that congregation is in serious trouble.

Tension as Normal

As you become familiar with the meanings of these four functions, you will begin to see them at work in your congregation. You also will notice points where one function will be at odds with another function. This is natural and to be expected. Tension is not necessarily a signal of church abnormality. Rather, it indicates common problems, predictable ones. The question, then, is how your church deals with them. Getting along with your pastor symbolizes many of the church's normal problems.

Your church's lifecycle is based on the four functions just explained. Now we will see how varying combinations of interaction between the four functions create the movement from one lifecycle phase to another. For ease of use, we will identify just four phases, a broad but manageable scheme.

LIFECYCLE PHASES: A FOUR-PART SCHEMA

As suggested already, the four basic organizations functions require attention in different combinations. This is because the *demands upon organizations shift as certain issues are met and others emerge.* These demands are predictable. A brand new organization differs from a long-standing one. Such differences are significant: they affect what organizations do, and how; they contribute to creation of its culture; and they guide how organizations get along with all of their constituents. Pastors are deeply influenced by the church's lifecycle location. This is why it is so important to be honest about where your church is currently located.

Let us now walk through an outline of these four lifecycle phases.

The Up-and-Coming Phase

Every organization starts somewhere, at some time. New companies or groups have little or no history upon which to draw; they depend upon the experiences, interests, beliefs, and commitments of the founder or founding cadre. By necessity, then, new organizations are forward looking; their prospects for survival depend upon achievement. They have to get out of the gate and do something. For this reason, the perform function tends to take center stage.

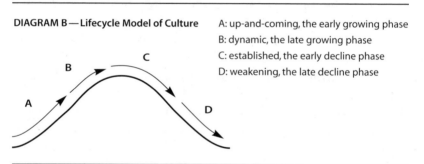

DIAGRAM B—Lifecycle Model of Culture

A: up-and-coming, the early growing phase
B: dynamic, the late growing phase
C: established, the early decline phase
D: weakening, the late decline phase

What makes this lifecycle phase "up and coming," then, is the organization's need to prove itself. This does not mean some self-centered desire being fulfilled but rather a demonstration that the organization can do what it says it does. My eighth-grade band teacher used to say, "Don't talk about it; do it!" In this regard, the up-and-coming organization clearly is growing: it is very flexible, able to try new things without the weight of tradition. This flexibility comes with its own built-in risk. One major danger in this phase appears when the organization tries to do more than it can handle at the time, to do too much too quickly. Being a new organization is no guarantee of success or viability. Yet a new organization has to make it happen, has to deliver, must continue to perform something.

Balancing Act At the same time, the performing by itself does not make the new organization strong. The other three functions must be included, even though they will not get as much energy or attention during this phase. The *envision* function is what created the organization to begin with; now it plays second fiddle while the new venture concentrates on doing things. Also playing second fiddle is the *relate* function. Who will be or should be involved?—as group members, as customers or potential customers? as government or other regulatory agencies? These questions must be handled, even as the young organization concentrates upon accomplishing things. For churches, issues that affect the "relate" function are especially pertinent: since church members are volunteers, their commitment must be nurtured in order to be maintained.

So, where is the *execute* function in the early up-and-coming phase? It lags behind. Getting the company organized is a low priority when things have to happen, when deadlines have to be met, when people who are checking out the new organization must be satisfied with what they find.

Here is what the up-and-coming phase looks like. This oversimplified schematic indicates both the functional priorities and the consequent "function flow" of energy (see diagram C). The diagram suggests that the up-and-coming organization faces a few basic challenges that it must learn to handle constructively. One

DIAGRAM C—Function Flow in "Up-and-Coming":
Action, Energy, and Potential Relationships

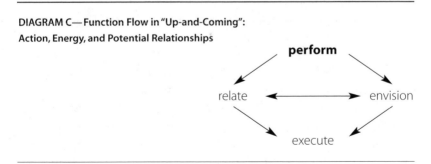

challenge is the danger of putting the proverbial cart before the horse. The purpose for which the company was established (envision) could get crowded out in the flush of success with doing things. This could thus endanger the venture's focus and sense of direction. Another challenge is in paying adequate attention both to constituencies and to developing strong, committed camaraderie (relate). This could endanger the creation of the kind of deep belief in group affinity that the organization needs in its cultural mud (see chapter 1). Affinity helps to overcome many challenges, as people who are committed to sticking together are more capable of figuring out their problems.[2] A third challenge in the up-and-coming phase is in neglecting the "execute" phase to a point where the company's resources are put in jeopardy. Burnout, lack of training, and limited cash flow can plague organizations in this earliest of lifecycle phases. The up-and-coming organization risks having eyes bigger than its stomach—seeking to do too much with too little.

Churches in the up-and-coming phase face all of these challenges and opportunities. They certainly must achieve results, as in regular, uplifting worship and other activities and programs that help the new church fulfill its vision. Getting such activities designed, scheduled, located, staffed, equipped, and under way takes a lot of time and energy. Most founding pastors and founding church cadres are eager to commit themselves to this kind of time and energy. When worship is going well and seeming to develop its own character and momentum, church founders can be tempted to focus on even more activity (perform). The other three church functions could get neglected. Relationships must be established as people visit, as new members join, as negotiations develop for use of physical space and other facilities, and so on (relate). Some attention to short-term efficiency (execute) is necessary as well. It reduces stress, frustration, and time for people to know who does what, how to use information, how the decision-making processes work, and the like.

Vision, Founders and Transition Perhaps even more importantly, *the founding cadre needs to continue to articulate and interpret the vision that is driving everything.* Repeating slogans that encapsulate the vision does serve a purpose and should not be discounted. However, any new group faces experiences and opportunities that it did not anticipate at first. Founders must be reflective enough to ruminate on such experiences in light of the vision. They likely will need to talk about the vision in expansive ways, to explain along the way—as they learn from their experience—what this vision looks like, now that "we are in the middle of things." The founding pastor serves the vision and the young church faithfully by engaging in such reflection and interpretation. Even more, the congregation will be stronger in the long run as the pastor shares this reflective interpreting with others. As it discerns God's continuing guidance for its life and witness, a congregation needs to learn that it can think together.

We realize, then, that the pastor's role in a young congregation can make all the difference. Especially when the pastor is the founder, the vision—and its cultural ramifications—is the pastor's to articulate and interpret. Up-and-coming churches with founders still in place must, to a large extent, negotiate their life through those founders' cultural lenses. If a church in this phase gets a different pastor, another danger lurks. The fledgling congregation's cultural mud is still being formed; will the new pastor honor what is taking shape there or seek different directions that would give the submerged material a different quality?

Toward the end of its up-and-coming years, the congregation must work through a major transition. This strenuous experience is necessary for preparing to move into the dynamic phase. Two primary tasks face the transitioning organization at this point. One task is to improve its disciplines of managing its day-to-day operations (execute). Here, key officials commit to developing processes that make it easier for the church to use its resources more efficiently, so that goals for the performing and relating functions are better met. Improving operations becomes detailed and tedious, but it will pay off.

The second transition task is about as different from operations as it could be. This task involves the vision. By this time in the organization's life, achievements are notable, but the organization's context invariably will have gone through some changes. The extent of these changes almost dictates the degree to which the vision must be adjusted. If the founder(s) do not encourage and cooperate with such a revision process, the organization might survive the transition, but it will not move into the dynamic stage. Instead, it will lose its chance for maximum vitality, sliding instead into an early process of decline.

In short, what you need from your pastor inevitably will change significantly by the end of this phase. Your church probably will not even realize that this transition is occurring; it could, instead, resist what is necessary. As a result, your pastor might become the victim.

The Dynamic Phase

Assuming that an up-and-coming church finds its way through the initial typical challenges constructively, it will move into the next phase. In the lifecycle model, this next phase is the one that the group wants to learn how to sustain. In other words, the dynamic phase is the goal, because it is the one that *utilizes all four organizational functions at their mutual strengths.* All organizations, including churches, should seek to become dynamic. It is in this phase, occupying only a small width along the lifecycle curve, that organizations are at their best. In basic theoretical terms, a church in this phase is balancing the strengths of both flexibility and self-management.

Organizations that reach the dynamic phase often are amazed at first at how well things are going. The focus and energy generated in this phase lead to high accomplishment. Organizations do better than they thought they could do. In church terms, this often means increases in worship attendance, program enrollments and participation, financial support, and general church spirit.

The function flow of energy has shifted from the way it looked in the up-and-coming phase. This is the congregation at its strongest (see diagram D). Here, organizations have a strong vision that drives everything else, so that the *other functions serve vision*, not the other way around. All of the church's activities and programs (perform) are connected well to constituent groups and work especially well because of its overall *esprit de corps* (relate). Procedures, management, and use of resources intentionally serve constituents and what the organization offers to constituents (execute).

DIAGRAM D—Function Flow in "Dynamic":
Energy from Vision Is Central

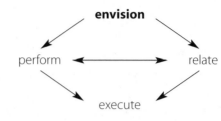

Pastoral ministry in the dynamic phase is, in many important respects, the most rewarding. Pastors who are fortunate enough to serve congregations in this phase (of which there are far too few—please note this point!) are usually experienced and skilled. They tend to have a lot of self-confidence and are highly regarded by their energetic and high-achieving congregation. For the time, everything seems to work like magic.

Yet, danger lurks even for the highly effective, dynamic organization. The most common occurrence for a dynamic organization is to move out of this phase. Such a movement occurs without members even realizing it. We will see in a moment that this move beyond dynamic signals the beginning of organizational decline. In lifecycle terms, it is very significant to recognize the irony of this development. When the organization finally has achieved the "top of its game," it tends to lose the edge that put it there. Remember: the relationship between organization and context is critical. While in the dynamic phase, the church is demonstrating its ability to take into account the world around it. A creeping complacence, however, becomes the church's enemy: it lulls it into giving context less and less attention. Hence, the church is in danger of choosing self-control over flexibility. Rather than staying fresh and dynamic, the church will slip quietly and easily into the early part of organizational decline.

If a dynamic organization can learn to detect its own natural proclivity for loss of vitality, it will gain a great advantage. It will be in an enviable position to review its world, polish up its vision, and make the kinds of adjustments in the other three functions, with the least amount of energy possible. Do most dynamic organizations do this? Unfortunately, no.

So, what happens instead?

The Established Phase

Most commonly, organizations do not sustain themselves as dynamic. They are lulled by an overinflated sense of accomplishment and security, believing that they are at the pinnacle and can remain there merely through repetition. It is as though the pastors, music minister, program staff, board members, and auxiliary presidents all gather in the church's nicest room one Sunday after worship. Everyone is smiling confidently and chuckling as the treasurer passes around a box of fancy cigars. Once they are all lit and the select body is puffing away, one of their company punctuates the occasion by stating aloud what everyone in the closed room is thinking: "Ahh, we've got it made!"

On Autopilot In spite of any idealistic religious protests to the contrary, I would argue that the spirit of this scenario depicts what happens, even to religious groups. Losing the vitality of the dynamic phase begins with a growing sense of congregational arrogance and complacence. Current achievements are viewed as so impressive that all the church needs to do is to keep doing what it is doing now. Once even a dash of this arrogance and complacence has pervaded the congregation, decline has begun. The established phase has arrived.

Lulling the church even further into its new self-deception, its measurable factors indicate continued success. To the untrained eye, high numbers for worship attendance, program participation, and financial support seem like ample evidence of a church in the dynamic phase. Early on, these can be deceiving, since the decline is just beginning, as the dropping curve on the diagram suggests. From the dynamic to the established phase, flow of energy between the four functions has changed again. The function flow now looks something like this (see diagram E).

An established institution increasingly focuses its energy upon internal matters. Satisfaction with perceived high success leads to more repetition of familiar activity and thus less innova-

DIAGRAM E—Function Flow in "Established":
Vision Waning, Networks Tightening

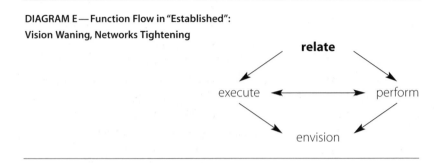

tion. Networks of relationships already in place grow in promi-
nence. Disagreements are handled behind closed doors. On the
surface, especially early, this decline looks like anything but decline. Vision, however, is losing vigor through lack of attention.
This means that the institution is more absorbed with its current
than with the near-future orientation that aided its ascent to the
dynamic phase.[3] As time goes by and environmental circumstances eventually make the organization's established and comfortable way of life much less tenable, dangers that once seemed
fully containable now threaten. They will surface most likely
over matters of staffing or finances.

Pastor as Manager Where is the pastor in an established-
phase congregation? Put more precisely, what parameters does
this phase of the lifecycle impose around the person in the pastoral role? One way to answer this question is to consider the
typical pastoral expectations of two generations ago. In the
mid-twentieth century, thousands of American congregations
already had existed for decades and were quite comfortable.
Their fairly stable memberships consisted of long-standing
members of various informal subgroups and subcultures, of
newer members finding their way, and of a satisfying number of
children and teenagers somewhat involved (relate). Worship
and other regular programs and ministries were all tried and
true; few new ventures were seriously considered (perform).
The current sanctuary and other physical facilities fulfilled the
congregation's space and aesthetic needs reasonably well; rou-
tines for finances and maintenance were quite familiar (execute). No one really talked about the church's purpose for exis-

tence: after all it had been around for a long time and survived, had it not (envision)?

In this kind of church setting, pastors direct traffic with activities, provide pastoral and crisis and care, juggle many demands on their time, and try to figure out how to satisfy the demands of the different congregational subgroups. Churches in this phase often seek primarily pastoral care, someone to meet their emotional and spiritual needs in time of crisis. This character of much church life was implied in the theological education curricula of the 1970s. Pastoral care and counseling was the rising star in courses for ministers in training; courses directed at the congregation as a whole were few and far between. An individualistic focus in church life suggests that the congregation is not self-reflective. The biblical and theological resources that pastors bring to the congregation often have been aimed at private experience and satisfaction, not the congregation as a community of faith created by the Spirit. Pastors, I would submit, often end up tired and yearning for energy to rise from the church itself. The church is more interested in a pastor who fits in than in one who invites them to wonder about God's Spirit seeking to blow afresh in their very midst.

Misplaced Epidemic *Decline seems to create its own momentum.* In one respect, it has been amazing to me at times to ponder the cultural mindset of churches who have lost their verve but do little about it. Church decline has become an epidemic in the United States. Tragically, this epidemic has not been clearly identified, so it is not well understood. Our attention over the last two decades has tended to be drawn toward church conflict—those episodes in our congregational life when disagreements and contests push themselves into the church's public arena. In many cases, conflict is a symptom of decline. We must learn to look more deeply than the presenting issue and details; conflict is a signal that something is afoot down in the church's cultural mud.

All too often, churches have few resources and even less motivation to address their early decline. All too often, churches find themselves caught off-guard by events that reveal how they are slipping. If churches do not face the truth about themselves, they continue to decline.

The Weakening Phase

Transitions from one lifecycle phase to another often occur unnoticed and certainly without fanfare. The differences between an organization late in the established phase and early in the weakening phase can be slight, almost undetectable. By this point, however, ongoing reductions in measurable features such as worship attendance, membership, participation levels, and budget have created an organization that is anemic and frail. Longstanding activities and procedures continue to be practiced, but they do not yield results as before. What marks entrance into the weakening phase is usually some event that evokes a crisis in the minds of church members. It might be disagreement over the performance of a key employee (such as the pastor) or curtailed income calling for significant cuts in budget, activity, and/or staffing. A public squabble ensues, dramatic consequences result, and then the organization tries to get back to business as usual. No one wants to talk about the conflict in public; the prevailing sentiment seems to be, "Let's just keep things going."

Now we are dealing with an organization that has become a shell of its former self. Very few new persons are joining; members are longstanding and getting old. They talk some about the organization's plight, but no one seems to know what to do. This is an organization that is moving along the lower right side of the lifecycle: it does not have too many options left. If it has to rely upon itself for sustaining resources, it also does not have too much time left.

When you ignore the world around you, you can last only so long. Not surprisingly, the function flow of energy in the weakening organization reveals another new set of interactions (see diagram F). What now dominates is attention to form, which means that what is done and with whom is less important than that "we do it this way." The question marks at the bottom of this diagram indicate that vision plays no part, that the weakening organization looks at the future only in terms of maintaining

DIAGRAM F—Function Flow in "Weakening":
Going through the Motions

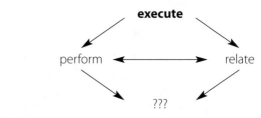

its past. It uses all of its resources, human and material, without any clear purpose except to survive. Desperation gradually seeps in. Church members want the pastor to save them, but God forbid that it would mean they would have to change!

Such a description is painful to read about (and no fun to write about, either!), but it reveals the kind of reality that thousands of organizations and churches have faced in recent years. As harsh as this account might sound, it serves a very valuable—and deeply biblical—purpose. In order to be fully faithful to our spiritual ancestors in the scriptures, congregations today need to learn to live with bad news in the good news. Congregations in the weakening phase ultimately must be able to speak the words in Ezekiel: "'Our bones are dried up, and our hope is lost; we are cut off completely'" (Ezek. 37:11). I am challenging churches across the country to face honestly and openly the truth about their situations. Only then can healing, renewal, and hope transpire. In New Testament language, the question for weakening churches then becomes, "What kind of resurrection do you want?" If churches in this phase will embrace their fear and uncertain future, then their pastors stand a chance of helping them discover new life.

In other words, the purpose of providing this model to a church audience is not to berate struggling churches—not to knock them down. The hope is, rather, that they will see that the seeds for renewal and vitality already live within the model itself. One of the lessons from lifecycle theory is that organizations should head somewhere and learn how to stay there. Churches—like other organizations—can learn how to reach the ideal dynamic phase and then sustain its vitality. Early in their lives, young organizations need to head toward the dynamic phase. Later in their lives, organizations need to recover the kind of energy and purpose that they are losing, by regaining their dynamism. The four functions hold the clues to revitalization. It is possible, it is desirable, and for churches, it is most truly faithful. But it takes deliberate attention, time, and energy to do so.

CONCLUSION: "WE HAVE MET THE ENEMY, AND . . ."

Reading through this chapter has required of you a willingness to concentrate and think. Like the other two cultural models in this book, the lifecycle is not simplistic. It requires sufficient learning to understand and apply. Church members who take the time to learn it discover a rich resource for helping their churches. When your church is better off, you are better prepared to get along with your pastor.

So . . . it all begins with you! Do the earnest but rewarding work of helping your church find its location accurately on the lifecycle. It is unrealistic to expect new pastors to figure you out on their own. As I have said, most congregations today are somewhere in decline. They have existed long enough to have noticed change around them but usually do not want to do anything about it. This puts your new pastor at a distinct disadvantage, even to the point of being set up for failure. If your "sayings" to a new pastor have do with things like attracting new members or starting a new ministry, your pastor will believe that you are ready to try something new. Will new stuff on the church's cultural shore bump into an old submerged belief? If you want your pastor's ministry with you to bear fruit, your church needs to answer questions like this for itself.

FOR REFLECTION AND ACTION

Use the descriptions of the four phases to do a "ballpark estimate" of where your church is currently located on the organizational lifecycle. Work with other members of your congregation. Keep in mind that the dynamic phase is easy to pass through and move beyond. Pay attention to how hard it is to be honest about your congregation's current characteristics. Be aware also of what kinds of fears might be stirred up; organizations on the decline side have a hard time being honest about their situations.

Below you will find lists of questions to ask yourself and your church, depending on which lifecycle phase your church currently occupies. These are questions that will require some thoughtful digging in order to get at the answers. Use these questions to begin serious conversations among yourselves about key issues affecting your church right now.

For all of the phases, these two questions about the pastoral role will be revealing:

+ What are the three most important things that your church wants from its pastor?
+ How does your current lifecycle phase help you understand why these preferences are what they are?

The Up-and-Coming Church

+ What does your church do well? How do you know?
+ With what it is still struggling?
+ In what areas is your church still able to adapt, to try new things?
+ In what areas is it becoming orderly and self-managed?
+ What is your church "learning" that it is beginning to take for granted?
+ How do visitors and members get involved?
+ How are problems being handled?

The Dynamic Church

+ What is your congregation's vision? How is it stated and shared? How does it motivate members and church groups?
+ How open, truly, is your church to new people?
+ What kinds of training are given to members?
+ How easily are new ideas tried out? What does it take to "drop" an activity?

- What is beginning to change in your community? How are you responding?

The Established Church

- What are your church's most important activities? How long have they been in place?
- How well do new members get involved? If you asked some active three-year members how welcomed they still feel, what might they say?
- Does the church governing board discuss and use the congregation's vision? Where is the congregation's energy?
- How hard is it to change a procedure, regular meeting time, budget process, paint color, and so on? Who makes those decisions and why?

The Weakening Church

- What did the church do ten years ago that it does not do now? Why?
- Who are the "key culture bearers" in the congregation? What happens if a new or younger member wants to try something new?
- What do church members talk about the most? When was the last "calculated risk" taken?
- Over what issue was the church's last disagreement? How was it "resolved"? Looking back, what submerged beliefs do you think were at stake?
- What is the congregation most afraid of? What has it done to address this fear?

✥ *three* ✥

FLOWING ALL AROUND YOU

Your Church's Streams of Culture

THE WORLD AT OUR FINGERTIPS

Have your travels ever taken you through a large international airport? It is quite an experience. The sheer size of things can be overwhelming: the expansive width of hallways, the distance between concourses, the height of ceilings in main buildings, the wing span of a double-decker passenger jet, the variety of food among the eateries, and so on. Furthermore, we encounter people from so many different places around the world. Every day, persons from Asia, the Pacific Islands, Africa, Europe, North America, and other locations carry bags, wear book packs, pull luggage, check in at gates, board jets of different sizes, and fly hundreds and thousands of miles to distant destinations.

Before the Internet, air travel was humanity's most dramatic way to recognize first-hand the great variety that is life. Just visiting an international airport reminds us, sometimes startlingly so, that it's a big world out there. Our limited awareness, however, do not mean that staggering diversity does not exist or does not affect us.

International airports and world travel help us connect to culture's presence and pervasiveness. They point out that culture is all over the place, literally. *Wherever human beings are, culture is.* Culture originates in many different sources that run into each other. What happens, then, when persons from different parts of the world meet? They face contrasts that must be acknowledged and respected if they are to interact as full social partners. We would expect this kind of challenge, for instance, between a Chinese village farmer and an English baroness.

CULTURAL STREAMING

Yet, is cultural distinction limited only to the most obvious features? This chapter answers that question with a clear but fascinating "no." We will explain a third way in which culture can be sliced, explained, and applied. The content of this chapter weaves around several claims. The first is that *culture also exists at various scales or sizes of streams, from small to very large, reflecting the various scales in which human communities exist.* The second claim is that *your church is influenced by elements from all of these streams.* This is another way of stating a point that was made in chapter 1, namely, that every organization is affected by what goes on around it. Culture is a strong influence, even when it seems invisible.

Third, *as streams of culture flow through society, they meet each other.* This meeting of the streams from many sources at one particular location is called *confluence,* a term borrowed from the study of nature to describe what happens when two or more courses of water come together. If one of them is larger than the others, it will dominate the resulting flow. The contents borne by the larger stream will tend to overshadow those of the smaller streams, in some cases breaking them up. This common phenomenon becomes a metaphor describing the intricacies of culture. Cultural confluence is taking place all the time, especially in the mobile world in which we live.

A fourth claim for this chapter is that *all of this confluent action creates idiosyncratic cultures within organizations, including churches.* The ways in which the various streams of culture meet in your church, the ways in which your church receives and responds to elements from them, eventuates in a combination of cultural elements in your church that is distinctly your own. Having said this, the other side of the point should also be clearly made. It is that *your church would not be what it is without cultural streams that exist beyond it.* To say that your church is "idiosyncratic" by no means implies that it has nothing in common with other churches. The concept of confluence allows us to recognize the presence both of identifiable influences outside of our local church and of the distinctive way that our church incorporates (or sometimes ignores) those influences.

What does all of this talk about cultural confluence have to do with your pastor? It means that your church has its cultural baggage, and your pastor brings some baggage, too. This is the fifth claim of the chapter. *Your pastor embodies a particular blend of cultural confluence as he or she joins you in ministry.* Much of what attracts you to your new pastor has to do with how your cultural confluences overlap. Yet, it is almost impossible for the overlap to be complete. Being aware of the places where difference exists should become a point of negotiation and creativity. All too often, however, churches respond to cultural "logjams" between themselves and their pastor in destructive ways.

Our last claim for this chapter is a logical consequence of the others. *The better that your church understands and deals with its current context, the better chance you have of getting along well with your pastor.* Most of the time (unless your current pastor founded the congregation), your pastors come to you as "outsiders" to your church. They are looking at you and your community with a fresh set of eyes, seeing things that perhaps you fail to notice anymore or value differently than your new pastor does. These differences of perception are grounded in different submerged beliefs that you and your pastor have. They therefore can become landmines, points of contention that gets lost in scuffles over the stuff on the shore of your church or community.

If your church understands its current context and is engaged in dialogue with it and about it, you are bringing a significant strength to ministry with your new pastor—a higher potential for identifying a common purpose. You and your pastor will be "on the same page" concerning your church's setting for its ministry. Cultural confluence then becomes a way to speak more deeply about mission opportunities: it offers a framework for interpreting not only the current life of the congregation, but also the world that is now facing you at your church's doorstep.

CONFLUENCE: AN EAGLE'S EYE VIEW

These six claims orient you to the focus and content of this chapter. As you might already see, streams of culture affect us ever so subtly but always inescapably. New terminology in the following pages will give you more details on this cultural theory. We will look at macroculture, six kinds of *mesocultures*, what a *microculture* is, and the presence of organizational (read here "church") culture, and acknowledge the intricacies of *subcultures* that exist at every scale. Consider this as well: every one of these streams of culture has its own swamp! They can be analyzed to their own depths, in their own muds. Yes, culture is indeed this rich—sometimes dizzying but always worth attending to.

So let us begin wading. We will work our way from the largest scale to the smallest. Pull up your pant cuffs!

MACROCULTURE: THE UNITED STATES, IDEAL AND ACTUAL

Our beginning point for confluence theory is with the social context that affects everyone who lives in North America, especially the United States. We will call it macroculture (see diagram G), using the Greek word *macro*, "large" to designate this broadest of cultural scales. American macroculture can be identified by particular stuff up on the shore of its swamp. Stories like the Pilgrims' first Thanksgiving with the natives, witch burnings, the Boston Tea Party, the American Revolution, removal of native tribes from their lands, major league baseball; documents such as the Declaration of Independence, the Constitution, and the Bill of Rights; practices such as Sunday picnics in cemeteries,

DIAGRAM G—Macroculture

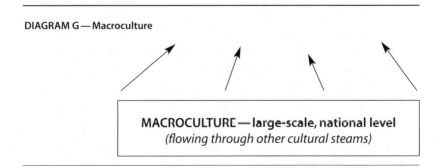

MACROCULTURE—large-scale, national level
(flowing through other cultural steams)

lynchings of African Americans, and Oktoberfest; places such as the Great Smoky Mountains, the Alamo, Las Vegas, and Mt. Rushmore; sayings in the water such as "Give me liberty or give me death," "manifest destiny," "freedom and independence," "states' rights"—these and many others associate us with a distinctive, broadly based cultural world.

Macroculture and Power

As you can tell, this cultural world grew out of a particular history, conventionally portrayed from the vantage point of those whose influence tends to frame the storytelling. Macroculture is that part of American experience that everyone who lives in the United States has to acknowledge, whether they understand it or not, like it or not, benefit from it or not. In other words, we must not automatically assume that macroculture supports and favors all persons equally. It takes little effort even today to identify chasms between those with opportunity and privilege and those who daily face limits to opportunity.

In terms from chapter 1, the swamp of American macroculture has its own submerged beliefs down in the mud. These beliefs are more powerful in any culture than its other two layers, the stuff or the sayings. In some cases, submerged beliefs contradict the very sayings that are publicly valued the most. Consider the right to vote as one macrocultural illustration. Early in American history, certain famous persons opposed popular elections. Instead, they wanted U.S. senators and presidents to be elected by state legislators—the elite. This does not sound consistent with "life, liberty, and the pursuit of happiness," does it? The "sayings" of young America (Declaration of Independence, Bill of Rights) have not changed, but their application has changed. The right to vote eventually has expanded from privileged white men to all white men to all men to all adults age 18 and older, men and women.

American voting rights provide one example of recognizing how macroculture exists, how it is complex, and how it changes. You don't have to like every macrocultural feature, but that does not mean that it will not influence you. For instance, I like shooting baskets and golfing, but I believe that most organized sports in America carry a zeal that overshadows even religion. I don't like what has happened to American sports, but it still is part of the macroculture in which I live.

Macroculture constitutes the bedrock of American society. Macroculture arches over every other scale of culture in the United States; it flows through all the other streams. This point is illustrated in Diagram G by the arrows, representing the flow of the macrocultural stream into others.

MESOCULTURES: VISIBLE AND INVISIBLE STREAMS GALORE

In between the pervasive influences of the American macroculture and the immediate experience of our particular local situation flow a number of other cultural streams. They are "in between," in the middle of the scales of cultural presence. For this reason, I have named them mesocultures, that is, cultures in the middle. We might not always notice middle-level cultures in our midst, but they are near at hand nonetheless. Their existence, and even resilience, account for many of the intricacies in our lives and communities. As we pay attention to mesocultures, we learn to appreciate the human handiwork of God in new ways (see diagram H).

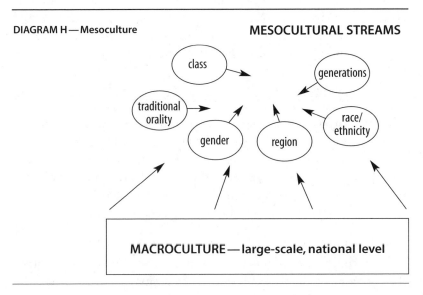

DIAGRAM H — Mesoculture　　　　　　　**MESOCULTURAL STREAMS**

class

generations

traditional orality

gender

region

race/ ethnicity

MACROCULTURE — large-scale, national level

In my rumination on the complexity of American society, I have differentiated six categories. These six guide our capacity for analyzing what goes on around us in terms of cultural flow at any given place. The categories are class, traditional orality, gender, region, race/ethnicity, and generations. We consider them here in no particular priority.

Class

I first began thinking about the culture of class as I traveled in my work.[1] When jets take off and land at airports, they very often are surrounded by particular patterns of human habitation. It didn't matter whether I was flying into Cleveland, Denver, Detroit, or another American metropolitan area. From the air, suburbs looked like suburbs, malls looked like malls. Modest-looking suburbs all looked the same, and fancy, upscale suburbs looked the same. This visual comparison led me to realize that there is a stream of culture in American society that expresses human distinctions between levels of material resources available to particular groups of people.

We are talking here about social class. We recognize that not everyone in America at any given time has the same equal status and certainly not the same amount of material resources. These differences are commonly distinguished by such terms as "middle-class," "upwardly mobile," "working class," "underclass," and so forth. What the cultural spin on class does is to highlight how these economic categories have effects not just on social standing but on cultural experience.

For instance, from our imaginary seat on the jet, we could observe two different suburbs. Imagine that, besides what we see from the air, we could hear residents in those respective communities talking about what is important to them. Differences in the visible trappings and differences in the values that are spoken aloud together suggest variations in the cultural mud of various social classes. Without judging them, we can learn to recognize that class exists indeed—and that it affects our churches.

Traditional Orality

Among the great variety of cultural expressions that fall within the category of class, one in particular deserves further attention.

It is actually a cluster of cultures in the United States that often is scorned and dismissed, yet continues to persist. My appreciation for this cluster of cultures was quite limited until I read one small book that opened my eyes. Tex Sample's book *Ministry in an Oral Culture* helped me see a lot of myself in the stories that he tells about himself.[2] Sample argues in his book that "traditional orality" is a term that encompasses many forms of human community life today, all around the world. Some of these forms still exist in the United States, where people learn to read and write, but their way of life is not defined by the methods of thought that "literate" culture deems essential.

What is at the heart of all oral cultures, Sample continues, are three basic characteristics. *Proverbs* are a primary means for teaching the community's wisdom and recalling it when an occasion calls for it. They distill what generations have learned about living and pass on that learning to the youngsters. *Storytelling* shares experiences out of the lives of the people, sometimes humorously, sometimes soberly but always as a way to affirm the world as the people live in it. *Relationships* are the glue that sustains the oral culture community. Decisions of all kinds are made on the basis, not of some abstract set of principles, but of considering the effect of what will happen to everyone in that community. Sample takes pains to emphasize these characteristics and show how they shape the lives of oral culture peoples.

One of Sample's points is that traditional orality is alive and well in American churches, because it is still very much a part of American society. It can be found in rural areas, small towns, working class city neighborhoods, and urban areas that are economically and socially distressed. Your church probably has clear evidence of this form of culture, regardless of its educational levels or incomes.

Gender

In society, males and females are treated differently. Typically, boys are encouraged to be assertive and dominant, while girls are trained to be passive and submissive. While there certainly have been individual exceptions to these stereotypes, we can still recognize these pervasive attitudes. Gender social differences arise from the cultural mud of virtually every known cultural stream—macro-, class, oral, and others. For much of human history, these demarcations of role probably were the most realistic way for human communities to survive. In recent generations, new ideas, pioneering experiences, and rapid technological development have rendered many of these gender-driven behaviors much less necessary.

Today in the United States and many other nations, women can enter pretty much any occupation they choose. Girls and women have their own athletic teams at schools and universities, with scholarships. Boys grow up to be nurses, interior decorators, and executive assistants. With all of these changes in the stuff on the shore of American macroculture, with the persistence of recent sayings in the water about equality between men and women, what do you think has happened to the submerged beliefs down in the mud?

For churches, gender culture is most evident in changes and controversies concerning ordination and the pastoral role. *Churches often mirror society in their own practices.* Women could become Christian educators because they worked with children. Many denominations today now formally approve ordaining women, but the actual experience of ordained women suggests that some things have not changed. The mud of many congregations holds submerged beliefs from an earlier era. Many women pastors feel called by God but not affirmed by congregations. Gender culture illustrates how culture can both change and resist, how new forms of a stream of culture can take root in some parts of society but not in others.

Region

In the 1960s, the popular Beach Boys band released a song called "California Girls." It compared California women to those from other parts of the country—from the East Coast, the Midwest, and the South. In its own way, "California Girls" illustrates another form of mesoculture. It is one that identifies behavioral distinctions based upon region of the country.

Regional mesocultures exist in the United States. I grew up in the West, lived in four of its states, then moved to the Midwest and, after a number of years, to the Southeast. These are three of the four basic regions that often are used in everyday conversation. The differences associated with regions create a set of mesocultural streams that run through American life in many various ways. People who were born and raised in the more rural South do tend to take life at a slower pace, to exhibit hospitable behavior to strangers, and to be polite. People who were born and raised in the more urbanized North tend to be in a hurry, to express their opinions readily, and to behave somewhat brusquely.

Such characterizations do not mean that everyone in one part of the country is exactly the same. It does suggest, however, that *any community's patterns of perceiving and engaging the world emerge out of its specific experience.* What happens to regional differences as millions of residents in the United States now move from one part of the country to another? Migration southward continues, as cities like Phoenix, Charlotte, Houston, Dallas/Forth Worth, Atlanta, and others grow in size. Whenever traffic congestion makes the news, someone is sure to blame the heavy volume and fast driving on "those damn Yankees!"

How do regional mesocultures affect your congregation? A Baptist denomination with many congregations in one particular southern state decided several years ago not to pass on pastoral applications to their churches if the pastor was from the western United States. It seems that a number of their churches had called pastors from western states, only to experience unexpected struggles in the relationship. Rather than try to help the churches change some submerged beliefs that they had inherited from living in their region, this Baptist official decided it was easier to stop the flow from the other cultural stream.

Not every meeting of regional cultures has to end in a logjam, but the point about potential clashes is valid. It can be applied anywhere that two or more streams of culture meet. In today's world, all kinds of streams meet just about everywhere.

Race/Ethnicity

Perhaps the most obvious and painful set of American mesocultures are those associated with race and ethnic heritage. They are obvious in the sense that they are fairly noticeable, having been associated with skin pigmentation and physical features. They are painful because the United States continues to wrestle, as it has throughout its history, with harsh discriminatory practices based upon designated definitions of what qualifies as acceptable ethnic/racial lineage. The civil rights era forced those of us who are white to look more seriously at the sometimes hidden effects of segregation and discrimination. These struggles are not limited to skin color. Jewish and Irish communities, for example, suffered poor treatment in the United States for generations after their first immigration as they gradually became relatively assimilated and acculturated.[3] Becoming aware of the presence of racial/ethnic mesocultures helps us acknowledge how they have been used as one dividing line for privilege.

We are speaking of the heavy side of this set of mesocultures, of their tragic histories in the United States. We do not want to be so weighed down, however, by the dreadful aspects of the past that we are not able to take another look. Every racial and ethnic mesoculture possesses its own richness. Most of them have origins in a macroculture from another country, as today's custom of identifying one as "African American," "Irish American," "Asian American" and the like attests. Further, not every ethnic group in the United States is one of "color." White ethnic groups immigrated to this country for many decades, from virtually all of the European nations and elsewhere—Germany, Norway, Russia, Poland, Italy, Austria, and so forth. Just because they were white, however, did not mean that they necessarily were welcome. Jane Addams labored in Chicago in the decades spanning the nineteenth and twentieth centuries, providing resources and assistance to all sorts of mostly European immigrants whose living and working conditions bordered on subhuman.[4]

The stories, traditions, customs, celebrations, observances, and so on, of each mesoculture speak of a peculiar communal in-

tegrity within each one. Alex Haley's popular book of the 1970s, *Roots,* demonstrates what happens when a community is uprooted and given little opportunity to sustain itself with familiar and treasured folkways. All of us came from somewhere, and most of our own roots are humble ones. Today's social emphasis upon "pluralism" provides communities a way to enrich their public squares, rather than to diminish the lives of certain others.

It will be hard work, though. Most of our churches are *mono-ethnic;* they consist of people from the same ethnic background, or people who have achieved a similar enough social status to be comfortable with each other. Many of the challenges to twenty-first century churches will appear in racial/ethnic garb.

Generations

The last of the six sets of mesocultural streams to be described in this chapter is the one made famous by the "baby boomers." Popular media have reported for years about what the baby boom generation has done to American society. They protested the Vietnam War, marched in civil rights demonstrations, dropped out of middle-class life, dropped back in and helped change American business, married, divorced, remarried, half-raised their children, and now are expecting everything that life has to offer. Their children, the "baby busters," also called "Generation X," do not view life as securely or hopefully as do their boomer parents. Busters seem to have little in common either with their boomer parents or their grandparents from the "silent generation." "Silents" came of age during World War II and entered the economic and social worlds as Europe and the United States set new records for output and profit.

Boomers, GenXers, and silents represent pieces of the puzzle that comprise theories about generational mesocultures.[5] Certain age groupings within the American population represent distinguishable patterns of life experience, value, and behavior. Generational "cohorts" share common effects from social mood, macrocultural trends, and events with national significance. Cohorts are clustered in about twenty-year eras; baby boomers, for instance, typically are designated as those born between

1946 (as GIs returned home from World War II and began having children) and about 1965, the first year since 1946 when the total number of American babies born in one year dropped.

Generational theory asserts that every generation approaches the world in some reaction to the previous generation, and boomers have been taken aback by such reactions. As the years have gone by, GenXers as young adults see the world differently than their mid-life and aging boomer parents. As their silent-generation grandparents die off, GenXers are willing to join the armed services in defense of freedom, but they want all the creature comforts. They often continue to live at home and bring to the workplace an expectation of defining employment on their own terms.

What generational theory helps the church to understand, then, is that *differences between age groupings are real; they create differing ways of valuing life and faith.* I remember as a teenager and young adult hearing older church members talk about my generation rebelling against church. "They'll be back when they marry and have children," was the usual response. What the latter did not anticipate is that the boomer generation's defining experiences were different than those of their parents. The same is just as true for GenXers. There are cultural reasons why we have a hard time identifying with people in another generation.

This realization should become a starting point for serious conversation in congregations about their future. How can a church sustained by the silent generation and yearning for its boomer children begin to attract young GenXers?

MICROCULTURE: SMALL IN SCALE, BUT MIGHTY IN EFFECT

Our introduction to the scales of confluence theory is nearing completion, but the last set of concepts certainly is not trivial. It is at the scale of local, lived experience that all of us encounter the dynamics of all the cultural streams. This local scale is smaller, "micro" in size, but it is like the pot where all the ingredients for the stew end up. All the larger streams of culture meet in specific, circumscribed settings. How do they get along? It all depends. In this section, we look at the basic elements of microculture. They become your tools for figuring out whether, in your church, you are experiencing cultural logjams or smooth sailing (see diagram I).

DIAGRAM I — Microculture

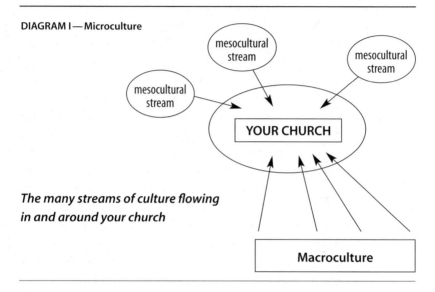

The many streams of culture flowing in and around your church

Generic Microculture

Overarching all small-scale cultures is the local unit, which could be a town, a rural county, or a city neighborhood. This is the place where all the streams from American macroculture and the several mesocultures meet, in some particular blend. That blend is your church's direct cultural context, out of which it lives. As we have seen already, if that context has changed significantly, your church could be in trouble.

Your primary microculture, then, is the one generated within the vicinity of your church's physical facilities. How much space this vicinity takes up depends upon the nature of your immediate community. By gathering some basic information about it, your church can stay tuned into factors that affect it most.

Organizational Microculture

An even smaller version of microculture is exhibited by groups with a history. Your church tends to mediate its experience of "the outside world" through its community's microculture. Variations between yours and theirs have been worked out through some level of awareness in your church that such variations are the ways that "we are different."

To explain further, begin with the middle of diagram I. Your church is represented by the rectangular box that sits inside of the oval representing your church's neighborhood. For the most part (although not entirely), your community microculture mediates all the mesocultural and macrocultural streams (represented by the arrows piercing the oval). It acts as a cultural filter (through its particular swamp mud—chapter 2), sort of like the way a water filter screens out certain elements. Thus, the versions of macroculture and mesoculture that the church experiences tend to be those versions that the church receives from its microculture. Your church then also does its own cultural filtering. Some elements flow in as fully as they were received; others get filtered, because they do not "get by" the submerged beliefs in the church's cultural mud. This process occurs in a complex manner, and its operation is mostly hidden from our conscious awareness (submerged materials are not readily available to our thinking).

Logjam Dangers

These subtle but powerful cultural relationships are easy to illustrate. Think of the many Korean congregations that have been established in the United States since 1980. Most of them were founded by immigrants who grew up Christian in Korea. Many of their original members are well-educated, middle-aged, and with professional job experience. Learning English is difficult, however; worship is conducted entirely in Korean. The congregation is a haven for maintaining traditions from home and for supporting new arrivals to America.

As the church's children grow up, however, they are less interested in speaking Korean at church. They want to sound and look like their English-speaking friends at school. Women go to college, find professional jobs like the men do, and seek more responsibility in church life. Any and all of such changes from the first years of immigrant life tend to challenge the congregation. These challenges might feel very local and specific, but confluence theory helps us to see the bigger picture. The microculture in this congregation is encountering another series of complex interactions between itself and other scales of culture. These interactions rarely go smoothly.

Even if your church is not Korean, you should be able to recognize in this sketch a story line or two that feels familiar. *Issues of gender, generation, class, race, and so on certainly affect your church.* These streams of culture meet at your church doors, whether they appear in subtle or confrontational forms. What gives your or any other congregation its distinctiveness, its "idiosyncratic" quality, derives from how these streams blend in your midst. Micro-, meso- and macrocultural influences together take a shape within your congregation that helps make it what it is, for benefit or ill.

What does all this talk about microcultures and idiosyncrasies have to do with getting along with your pastor? Imagine that your pastor has come to you after having served three other congregations. The previous three all were about the same size as yours, in towns about the same size, with church members having similar backgrounds, experiences, and interests. You are both tempted to suppose, based on the superficial evidence of the "stuff on the shore" and the 'sayings in the water," that you are an ideal match. It might turn out that way—blessings on all! But how well do you know each other, really? What places in your church's cultural mud might there be a submerged belief that will throw your pastor off?

Cultural confluence becomes an illuminating tool for helping you anticipate the dynamics of dancing with your new pastor.

Subcultures

One final category rounds out the cultural confluence theory. It is a category that is most easily recognized at the level of organizational microculture, but applies across other scales as well. Subculture refers to something that is nested inside something else: "Simply stated, a subculture is a culture that has formed within a host culture, sharing some of its assumptions (read "submerged beliefs") but developing others (some of which are contradictory to the host) of its own."[6] For example, mesocultures are subcultures of American macroculture; microcultures are subcultures of their regional subculture; and so on. One of the most common subcultures in churches emerges out of its choir or choirs. I have heard and witnessed enough contests between choirs and clergy to know that there are landmines a-plenty when the pastor goes messin' with the music! Other subcultures often develop with the women's auxiliary, the youth ministry, Christian education, the board of trustees, the deacons, and other subgroups.

There is nothing wrong with subcultures per se; the problems arise when a particular bit of stuff symbolizes something positive to one subculture and something negative to another. Not only this, but, once a church has begun its organizational decline, one of its subcultures becomes dominant. Longtime members will sense the dominant subculture's influence and who represents it most forcefully. It does not help your church when your pastor runs into a brick wall with the dominant subculture. It is to your church's advantage to help your pastor find his or her way among the fascinating, rich, yet sometimes bewildering world of cultural idiosyncrasy that is your congregation.

CONCLUSION AND TRANSITION

We have now journeyed our way through three cultural models that you can use with your church. I am hoping that the discussions in these last three chapters have spurred your thinking about how to see your church—and your pastor—through these cultural lenses. In part 2 of the book, our application will be directed toward a specific list of topics bearing upon your pastor and you. Some of these topics were chosen in part because they are "hot-button" church issues these days. Other topics commend themselves to us because they are culturally laden but often get treated lightly or bypassed altogether. My intent by the end of part 2 is to have discussed these topics with you in such a way that you are "ready to roll" and can apply them in your own situations.

Before you begin reading the chapters in part 2, I invite you to take a few minutes first for review. Think over each set of questions listed as "For Reflection and Action" in the chapters of part 1. They will reinforce your learning, assisting you to look at your congregation and its pastor from a new perspective. As Dorothy said upon reaching Oz, "We're not in Kansas anymore!"

See you in part 2!

FOR REFLECTION AND ACTION

• What categories would you use to identify all the forms of diversity that exist in a five-mile radius from your church's front doors? What do those categories suggest about the purpose of your church's current mission?

• Which streams of culture are most present in your church (that is, regional, racial/ethnic, class, micro-, etc.)? How did they get there? How do they compare with your neighborhood or town?

• Which members of your church are most identifiable with which "outside" streams of culture? How might these various streams be influencing members' behaviors?

• Which streams in your church's organizational culture does your pastor need to understand most? Which streams does she or he exhibit that are not evident in your church's culture?

• With which streams of culture in your community's micro-culture is your congregation least familiar? How might this limited understanding be affecting your congregation's ministry, especially in outreach?

Part Two

GETTING ALONG
WITH YOUR PASTOR

In the first part of this book, you read about culture as a theory that you can use in your church. You were introduced to three ways to frame culture, three sets of concepts that overlap with each other. Together, this culture theory becomes a lens through which you see your church and your pastor. Culture helps you become aware of things that you might otherwise miss.

In the second part of this book, you will read about how culture helps you do ministry with your pastor more effectively and wisely. Rather than identify and discuss a wide range of topics, part 2 limits the conversation to four key issues:

- How you welcome your pastor and make a place for her or him at your cultural table
- How culture is a form of church power that your pastor needs to learn how to use and of which your pastor must become a part
- How to understand conflict and train your congregation to respond to it very differently
- How culture influences what leadership looks like and how leadership acts

As you continue reading, be aware that you are still learning to think about your church with a new model. You likely will shift back into your familiar ways of thinking about this subject without even realizing it. Allow part 2 of the book to keep reminding you that this new model will take some time to learn. Treat the practical applications in these chapters as they are intended to be used—as gospel-driven, fruitful ways of church behavior, derived from a fresh way of seeing what is going on.

four

BECOMING A HOSPITABLE HOST

Pastoral Adoption as Welcome and Discovery

THE STRANGER BECOMES A PASTOR

He was a small-town kind of guy, and they were in the city. He
had grown up on a farm; they had worked in factories, taught
school, run businesses. He was used to church buildings made
out of wood, surrounded by quiet lanes with no sidewalks,
where children rode their dusty bikes after school until dusk.
Their sanctuary was one of the few in the country with windows
designed, built, and installed by Tiffany.

When he became their pastor, I wondered if this match-up
would work. They had been accustomed to a little glitter and
pizzazz, and the Rev. John Dixon, DMin, clearly had neither. To
be honest, their downtown community had become abandoned,
and the stunning homes across the street turned dingy, harboring
desperate people looking for shelter or a momentary thrill. Their
membership numbers had been dropping for twenty-five years.
What would a quiet, young pastor with facial scars and a limp
and a proud, aging congregation with a Dun and Bradstreet past
have in common?

In Rev. Dixon's first year as their pastor, the small congregation suffered sixteen deaths. These church members had been
pillars of a church once grand and now teetering back against
the ropes. John officiated at all of the funerals, leading each one
with dignity, celebrating the life and Christian witness of each
one of these faithful members. It was a tiring first year for the

young Rev. Dixon, and for the struggling church as well. The deceased all were key culture-bearers, John realized. The future of the congregation would be different without them.

When he had first arrived, he knew that this new call would require dealing with some tough decisions. The church was holding on, to its proud history, to its unique and beautiful building, to its fellowship across the years. Rev. Dixon knew that it would not, that it could not, last much longer.

By the end of John's third year as pastor, the congregation had decided to move. It had not been an easy decision to make, but John walked them through the process all the way. His quiet demeanor; his love for the people; his listening to the stories, hopes, and fears; his acknowledgement of the historic facility that they would be leaving—these were many of the ways that Rev. Dixon used his pastoral role to help the church make a very crucial decision. Five years later, the church was being transformed. On a growing edge of their town, with young families moving in, with money in the bank from the sale of their cherished building, this congregation was beginning to breathe in new life. John had led them through the wilderness, and they had come to trust his guidance.

ANATOMY OF GETTING ALONG

How did it come about that a congregation and a pastor with so little in common could live together and take such a big step? Rev. Dixon's pastoral style—quiet, calm, attentive, supportive, soothing, inviting—would have been at work in his first year, no matter what events had occurred. Yet, because of the crisis brought about through so many deaths so soon, Rev. Dixon and the congregation were thrust upon each other. They found out rather quickly what each other was like under stress. This could have been a breaking point, since stress tends to threaten the congregation's submerged beliefs, especially the fragile ones (see chapter 1).

In the providence of God, the sixteen funerals in twelve months gave the church and its pastor an opportunity to bond. What was key was that the church saw in Rev. Dixon's actions (honoring the stuff on the cultural shore) and words (affirming the sayings floating in the cultural water) a care for them and a deep interest in their welfare and future. In other words, this is a dramatic story about *pastoral adoption*. At some point, the congregation—however intuitively, unconsciously, or informally—extended itself to John. He had proven himself capable and worthy to be their pastor. Their actions and words to him were a necessary part of the dance that creates adoption. *Without its own congregational way of saying, "You are one of us," the adoption process would be incomplete.*

HOSPITALITY: THE FLIP SIDE OF ADOPTION

It would be tempting for church folk to assume that all the responsibility for good working relationships between pastors and churches falls on the pastoral side of the equation. Do not be deceived: there is a critical role that you as congregation must play if your pastor is to gain the kind of *cultural capital* that your church knows and regards as worthy. Cultural capital refers to those particular elements of power and influence anchored in the congregation's own culture (stuff, sayings, and especially submerged beliefs) that persons and groups can acquire and use as they become accepted and trusted. Cultural capital is a commodity that is generated out of your church's idiosyncratic life and the culture that is created as a result. Over time, a number of members gain more cultural capital than others, even between one part of the church's life and another. It is a significant form of power, and its use within the congregation determines its benefit or detriment.

Cultural capital is closely tied to pastoral adoption. Without the pastor gaining sufficient and appropriate cultural capital, your church's pastoral ministry is in jeopardy. Certainly, the pastor carries some responsibility in this adoption process. This is a coin with two sides, however. The congregation's way of interacting and responding to its new pastor influences the pastor's ability to gain cultural capital. In particular, the way that your church can help this process along is as a welcoming host to the new stranger. If they are to be accepted and thus useful to the host community, strangers must receive heartfelt hospitality. Offering this hospitality is your task with any new pastor.

BIBLICAL MUSINGS

Hospitality as a congregational practice has many biblical precedents and much theological support. In Ephesians, Paul explains what has happened, in light of the gospel, between the historical chosen people of God and those nations outside of God's elect. In Paul's day, descendants of the biblical Israelites believed that the promises of God applied only to those born into their community. These other nations, the Gentiles, thus were "far off" (2:13), "strangers to the covenants of promise, having no hope and without God in the world" (2:12). The work of Jesus Christ changed all that. The peoples who have been at odds with each other, one seen as inferior to the other, now become "one new humanity in place of the two" (2:15). Gentiles now "have been brought near" (2:13) through Christ. As a result, all the former language of exclusion no longer applies. The offer of full life in Christ comes to all nations, all peoples. They are "no longer strangers and aliens, but . . . citizens with the saints [believers of Jewish descent] and also members of the household of God" (2:19).

It seems to me that the practical, daily life implications of Paul's explanation often get lost in churches today. In God's eyes, because of what Jesus Christ stands for, believers who feel that they have the inside track with God are no better than those who used to be on the outside. If this is true for God, what does it look like among us? How do churches welcome strangers, that is, persons from communities who have been viewed as left out of God's grace?

In one of its earliest narratives, the Hebrew Bible has preserved an episode from the story of Sarah and Abraham that suggests the role that being hospitable can play in the purposes of God. The couple had been called by God to leave their home and travel to a new place, to establish a new community that would further God's intentions for the world (Gen. 12:1–9). Because they were old and had no children, they wondered how this promise could be fulfilled.

One hot day during their journey, their party was joined by three other travelers. The text, Genesis 18, goes into some detail at this point to show how eager Abraham and Sarah were to play good hosts to these strangers. They threw together a top-rate menu, and Abraham himself served them the meal. Once they were fed, the guests made an announcement: Sarah would have a baby a year from then.

This news was unexpected, to be sure. Sarah and Abraham were old, "senior citizens" as we might say today. Yet it was not simply the promise of childbirth that excited the elderly couple. It was the hope that they would begin to see God's original promise to them come to pass. Even more, the story suggests that our behavior can have significant consequences.

In a fascinating yet undogmatic way, this story links together divine promise with possibility. The story does not leave us with a simplistic message that being nice to strangers sets in motion some cosmic energy that will favor us. Abraham and Sarah's encounter with the men at the trees symbolizes something else. They showed respect to strangers who were traveling in the desert—dusty, weary, thirsty, and hungry. We can only speculate on Abraham's and Sarah's inner feelings or motivations at the time. What we read is of an elderly couple on a journey of their own, offering hospitality to strangers, hosting with generosity, receiving news that was both unexpected and wondrous.

If the biblical ancestors of our faith extended hospitality to those who brought surprising and amazing good news, how much more can we today hear the call to become hospitable churches?

YOUR PASTOR AS STRANGER—YOUR CHURCH AS HOST

Hence, *a key factor in your church learning to get along with its pastor is your hospitality.* Congregational acts of welcome, kindness, and generosity strengthen the possibility for a strong pastor-church relationship. Hospitality becomes your church's part of the adoption formula. It can set in motion the quality of experiences and relationships that will benefit your ministry.

Pastoral adoption is a process akin to a stranger appearing in the midst of your community.[1] Your church is the host, not unlike Abraham and Sarah hosted the three strangers. If the stranger stands a chance of moving toward acceptance by the community, she or he must be received with gestures of hospitality. In other words, the *host* (church) needs to treat the *stranger* (new pastor) like a welcome guest. Rituals, ceremonies, and other acts of generosity on the part of your congregation become your opening reception. You are trying to communicate that you are willing to "give it a shot," to meet the pastor halfway, to do what you can to make the new relationship work well. Certainly, the pastor (guest) must receive your gestures with gratitude. He or she will do so out of a posture of humility, acknowledging through word and action that he or she relies upon your hospitality to get settled in and begin to share your way of life.

So, then, the pastor ideally behaves as a humble guest in your house, but your church as host realistically has apprehensions. What does he want from us, and what does she bring to us? There will be a period after the initial welcoming during which you still will be wondering. You know that your new pastor bears gifts, and some of them are yet unknown. Until you trust your new pastor, you are not sure how you will negotiate those new gifts and your community's life.

HOSPITALITY AND ADOPTION: BY THE PHASES

A pastor who feels genuinely welcomed by and in the congregation is in a better position to serve you. Simply put, this is the goal of your hospitality—the pastor's adoption into your church's life and ministry. It is important, therefore, that your church learn how not only to welcome the new pastor but to live with whatever level of uncertainty or insecurity his or her presence brings to the new situation. We will pursue this task using all three culture models, framing this discussion with the lifecycle phases.

Up and Coming Church

A young, growing, flexible, and reasonably accomplished congregation often does not get a new pastor. The tendency of "starter" churches is for the pastor who helps found it to stay for a long time. In some traditions (Baptist, Pentecostal, and other), the pastor very well could stay for life. In other traditions, where the denomination is involved in supporting new church development, the pastor who founds the church might stay for five to seven years and then either be appointed elsewhere or accept another call.

We know that organizations in the up-and-coming phase are still growing. They are more flexible, more supple and lithe, than they are self-managed or rigid. The church as a whole is better capable of trying new things. In terms of the cultural swamp, the church's culture is still being created. All the cultural streams represented by the founders and members are being tested in the church's experience. Usually the founding pastor's submerged beliefs—as well as his or her preferred "stuff" and "sayings"—are the most influential.[2] Conflict could arise when these three cultural levels do not appear to the young church to be consistent. Otherwise, an up-and-coming church is in a strong situation overall to receive a new pastor.

What helps a church in this phase is to continue to be proactive. One of the basic features of healthy hospitality and pastoral adoption revolves around *communication*. The church's governing board can set the tone, with written and spoken comments about the new pastor. The board also can help by setting up regular opportunities for board members, staff, and officers of various church ministries to meet with the new pastor. It can make a big difference to the congregation for those charged with leadership to be talking frequently with each other and the pastor. Any concerns about her or his actions or words should be discussed right away and respectfully. Whatever process is used should be clear and aim to help everyone learn together.

Another feature of effective adoption involves events that help the congregation get to know its new pastor. By themselves, routine functions—of worship, preaching, visitation, and the like—do not endear the pastor to the congregation. It will help to organize events and activities that allow members, staff, and officers to be together with no official agenda:

- A reception following the new pastor's first Sunday of preaching
- A potluck supper including some light-hearted activities in which members and pastor can exchange gestures of welcome and goodwill
- Cottage meetings in several members' homes, where the pastor can listen to stories and dreams, as well as doing some sharing of his or her own
- A board retreat within the first six months, including recreation and fellowship but also free conversation about the church's current condition, hopes, challenges, etc.

Such occasions permit the kind of "checking out" the pastor in a nonthreatening way. Both parties can observe what is on the shore of each other's cultural swamps, as well as see what is floating in the water through the respective sayings. What is in the mud will take time to discern. More accurately, church activities with the new pastor offer some glimpses into what the new pastor might end up contributing to the church's still-forming mud.

An up-and-coming congregation eventually will face the need to rework its vision. This task probably should wait awhile. Discussions about vision, while appearing to deal with what is floating in the cultural water, ultimately affect what ends up in the mud. You want your new pastor to be known and trusted well enough so that such a central topic does not raise too much anxiety. You want your pastor to avoid snagging a foot on a submerged belief without knowing that it is there. Learning how to learn is a central challenge for any church that wants to stay faithful to the gospel but also beneficial in its witness. Before your new pastor has been with you too long, the "vision thing" should be a central item for the governing board.

A pastoral transition during the up-and-coming phase of a church's life provides significant moments for intentional learning. Remember, this is a very formative period. Even though the church has a short history and a swamp still under construction, it still could be setting the stage for its own early decline. Founders who are rigid about practices can embed in the congregation a low tolerance for flexibility. If your new pastor is following such a founder, the transition will be more challenging for both pastor and church. Any pastoral transition takes some time and energy to engage effectively. Listening skills, respectful discussion, open processes, and the like will help your church, even in the middle of its moments of uncertainty. Years from now, you want to look back at your church and realize that it learned a number of strong, adaptive submerged beliefs in its fledgling days.

Dynamic Church

Before saying anything about how a dynamic church hospitably welcomes a new pastor, a couple of qualifications are in order. First, the bad news: there are not that many of you out there. It takes a period of years to reach the dynamic phase, yet sustaining focus and fresh vitality is harder than it sounds. Most churches move right through this phase and begin decline before they know it, thinking that they are still dynamic. Second, the good news: the dynamic phase is not a time when pastors usually leave. Usually the pastor serving a dynamic congregation was at the pastoral helm as the church made this important transition. Things are going well enough that no one—not pastor, church board, or congregation—is thinking about a changing of the guard. The church needs a pastor who will help it to sustain its dynamic strengths, not fall into a rut.

For these reasons, the dynamic phase is probably the easiest one of the four in which a church could be adopting a new pastor. Its biggest danger is in slipping unawares into the established phase. This means a decreasing interest in staying fresh and flexible and an increasing interest in things as they are. Cultural mud thus begins to harden, ironically at the time when the church could adapt with high effectiveness. The pastor's primary task in the dynamic church is to help it learn how to sustain itself without falling into repetition and closed relationships. *Any changes that affect life in the neighborhood or community will threaten the strengths of the church's dynamic phase.*

To be proactive, then, means to *sustain the creative tension* in the church that makes the dynamic phase possible. The church's governing board needs to be committed to variations on its accomplished dynamic themes. Not everything can stay exactly as it is indefinitely and still maintain the dynamic interactions. A new era is being ushered in, not one that has to become completely different, but one that demonstrates that the church can remain fresh. Board members must learn to resist the temptation to be swallowed up in the details. They must talk among themselves about their readiness to create change. This readiness must be fostered within the congregation as well.

Activities such as those listed in the previous section can foster the congregation's readiness with its new pastor. Along the way, the pastor and board discuss what kind of "sayings" would be most helpful. Perhaps most of these sayings would be familiar to the congregation, but one or two of them might need to put a fresh spin on things. With the board's support, the pastor then *reinforces the sayings* through his or her behavior and statements (stuff on the shore). To be adopted, the pastor must reinforce familiar sayings and the practices (stuff) that are associated with it. The board and pastor establish a trusting, respectful relationship through *monthly review and evaluation in the first year.* The pastor initiates contacts with board members outside of formal meetings, to strengthen rapport and understanding.

A dynamic church might be somewhat oriented to tasks, so the adoption process could get short shrift. Remember that *your new pastor cannot be just a manager, if you expect your church to maintain its dynamic posture.* Be deliberate about your church's gestures, especially the public ones that are designed to show your hospitality to this new stranger. You want the adoption process to go well. If your new pastor faces congregational resistance, the ensuing tussles could trigger the church past the dynamic phase and into an early and unnecessary decline. Your church has a lot at stake at this point.

Established Church

Churches that have begun organizational decline usually do not know what is happening to them. On the surface, their situation looks enviable: worship, education, and other activities are continuing well; there is a recent history of accomplishment; physical facilities and funding are as adequate as ever; the congregation feels good about itself. So what is the problem? Early on, the church likely will not catch itself becoming more repetitious. This early part of the established phase intensifies a couple of phenomena, reflecting the movement out of the growing side and into the declining side.

One of these signals of decline at work is the appearance in the church of a *dominant subculture,* a segment within the congregation's culture that tends to wield primary influence. This dominant subculture often is recognized intuitively by many church members, in the form of a handful of persons who represent strongly the submerged beliefs peculiar to this subculture. Without saying it aloud, the church subgroup that has created this subculture believes deep down that its agenda is more important than any other. Dominant subcultures can become associated with the music department, the board of trustees, the women's auxiliary, or other church groups. The ways in which they exercise their cultural capital can vary, but often it occurs through informal channels. As a result, *the dominant subculture does not need a majority on the church's governing board in order to get its way.*

The second signal of decline at work explains why a dominant subculture does not need numbers to flex its cultural power. Every church at the beginning of decline has *key culture bearers,* members who, over time and participation, have won the respect and trust of the congregation. Most commonly, a key culture bearer supports the dominant subculture. As a congregation moves further into decline, these key culture bearers tend to push agendas that hurt the church's ability to recover from its decline. Sometimes they act as bullies in the church, less respected and more feared, speaking out on behalf of less vocal proponents of the dominant subculture. A less common key culture bearer is the one whose loyalty to and participation in the church is quiet yet recognized. This member often sees what is wrong in the church but is not of a personality to challenge those culture bearers of the dominant subculture.

Dominant subcultures and key culture bearers tend to symbolize a church in decline, especially as decline continues. Because of their unquestioning commitment to longstanding submerged beliefs in the church's mud, a dominant subculture and its promoters assume that "business as usual" is fine. As time goes by, however, this position is dangerous. Changes in population, in generational, racial, or ethnic composition of the community, in the economy, and so on eventually catch up to a church that is treading water. Those who are most loyal to the dominant subculture will hold on for dear life.

Forms of resistance typically employed by the dominant subculture include responding to new proposals in a lukewarm way. Later in the established phase, lukewarm response turns to opposition and, eventually, as the church becomes even weaker, into open conflict. Key culture bearers are convinced that they have the well-being of the congregation at heart. Since tried-and-true submerged beliefs represent to this subculture the church's best, it is no wonder that resistance to change becomes one of its potent strategies.

Why is this summary of resistance patterns important for you and your new pastor? It is because your new pastor often represents the potential for new possibilities. Churches in the established phase can be confused about what they want from a new pastor. They can say (cultural level: floating in the water) one thing about new members, new programs, and the like, all the while not being ready for any of the submerged beliefs (cultural level: down in the mud) to be challenged. A new pastor might suppose that the church is ready to make some changes, to welcome new people with new skills and interests. What the congregation (that is, its dominant subculture) really means is usually different. The church would like to have enough people to keep cherished programs going, with new folks taking over old jobs and supporting the church financially. As long as new people fit in, the established church will be happy. If they propose any new stuff on the shore of the cultural swamp, a contest could arise—and often does.

What kind of hospitality and adoptive strategies can a savvy established church initiate for its new pastor?

Keep in mind that, in every phase, we are seeking to equip church members to be proactive. Most churches have governing boards that are charged with congregational oversight, so it will be key to the adoption effort that the board take the lead. This does not mean that board members make all the decisions and do all the work behind closed doors. Rather, one of the board's wise moves will be to foster conversation among board members who represent the church's various subcultures. Without such means of dialogue, it is difficult to identify and affirm goals and activities that all groups affirm. Dialogue also encourages honesty about differences of interest and opinion. These differences could symbolize potential conflicts regarding the new pastor.

Since misunderstanding is more likely in the established than the dynamic phase, it will be especially fruitful to *define processes for the pastor's first year:*

- How will the pastor *communicate:* with the congregation as a whole, with board members, with staff, with outside constituencies?
- What kinds of *events and activities* will be planned and carried out to acquaint the pastor with the congregation's members and various groups and auxiliaries?
- How often and by what means will pastoral *performance* be appraised?
- What process will be utilized for handling any *tensions* about the pastor's activity?
- In which areas of church life can *changes* be negotiated, and which ones will be left "as is" for the time being?

By clarifying these kinds of processes, all parties in the new relationship stand a better chance of putting their best foot forward. Early organizational decline can send a church's new pastor mixed messages. She or he might hear interest for new things in one corner and satisfaction with the status quo from another corner. Without pandering to key culture bearers, the new pastor nonetheless needs to recognize the particular cultural capital in this church and how it works. If culture bearers truly care about the church, they understand that the pastor must acquire some cultural capital, too.

Church hospitality to a new pastor affords the established church's governing board an opportunity to learn. It can begin training itself to interpret the cultural complexities of its church. What do all the gestures of welcome stand for? In what ways might they symbolize either openness or resistance to change? Hospitality and adoption are essential steps in getting along with your pastor, but the challenges do not end there. Eventually, your pastor needs to help your congregation recapture the kind of vision clarity and energy for mission that has quietly slipped. To be effective, this task of recapturing must be undertaken skillfully.

Weakening Church

Hospitality and adoption in a weakening church have their own challenges. The congregation seeks an energetic wonder worker to pull it through its protracted slump and give it new life again. If ever there was a temptation to treat a new pastor like a savior, this is the moment! However, the congregation's submerged material in its cultural mud has become increasingly out of touch with its world. The cultural confluence that helped create this church is gone or appears as a shadow of years past. The congregation's energy level has been dropping for awhile now, leaving the surviving members with a defeatist attitude. Few, if any, teenagers, children, young adults, and newer members remain. Maintenance requires increasing attention to a shrinking and strained budget. The congregation often only can afford to pay a pastor who is inexperienced or elderly and part-time. Thus, the new pastor often comes to the church with much less skill and savvy than the church desperately needs.

Yet, in spite of all of its troubles, the weakening church needs to see its own hospitality as a step toward the future. If it wants to do more than survive long enough to bury the rest of its remaining members, *this congregation must view its new pastor as a link to new life.* That new life clearly will mean change, significant change. The hospitality and adoption process that it provides its new pastor becomes the church's way of preparing itself to embark on a journey into uncharted territory. Its new pastor becomes the struggling congregation's guide, a Sacajawea for the Lewis and Clark expedition. Lewis and Clark had to trust the young native woman to translate accurately the strange new world through which they trekked. Likewise, trust and respect must develop between the new pastor and the frail band of church members seeking a future and a hope.

Under these circumstances, adoption perhaps is at its most difficult. It will take more energy and intention to play out the embedded roles of pastor as stranger/guest and the church as host. Landmines abound deep within the shaky church's cultural mud. What basic strategies and tactics stand the best chance of helping this church adopt its pastor?

Hold a few events at the beginning of the pastor's tenure that help pastor and members meet, talk, and listen to each other. Your new pastor must learn to be an "ear" before acting as a "mouth."[3] She or he needs opportunities to listen to the congregation, to observe its life together, to hear what members have to say about their stories, their penchants, and their dreams. Be intentional, then: accompany your pastor to meetings and events of your church's auxiliaries; arrange for gatherings in which the pastor can mingle with and listen to members and officers alike. When it is the pastor's turn to speak, it should be about basic, casual things. Encourage your new pastor to emphasize an interest in caring for the congregation. It is organizationally weak; trust and confidence must be established before agendas to revitalize the church ever are discussed.

Tell the church's story, as painful as it will be in places, as thoroughly and as honestly as possible. There is no benefit in trying to hide your condition from your new pastor. If this new ministry relationship stands a chance of amounting to more than hand-holding, your pastor needs to know the score. What stories out of your past convey your congregation's greatest pride, as well as its deepest struggles and misfortunes? You might be embarrassed, still angry with previous pastors, and even still at odds among yourselves about more recent events and outcomes. Regardless of the church's desire that some of its history would somehow disappear, it is what it is—and it still affects you. Find a way to make peace among dissenting parties, at least in agreeing that the stories will be told. Just getting to this point can help give the church some of the strength that it needs.

Help the pastor channel her or his energy into relationships and activities that will build cultural capital. Longtime church members of a weakening church have more invested in it than newer members. Their cultural capital needs to be recognized and honored, even if some of it is based on a way of life that will not sustain the church much longer. Key culture bearers often behave as though they have a right to get what they want. The purpose of your new pastor building trust and respect among longtime members as a whole is not to take his or her marching orders from them. *Resistance to change is strongest in the church's subcultures that have the most to lose with change.* The more cultural capital your new pastor can accrue with longtime members and key culture bearers, the better chance the church has to deal with necessary change constructively.

Discuss candidly but respectfully the congregation's fears, Telling "the whole story" that culminates in the congregation's current condition is hard enough work. Any organizational change process that works begins with truth-telling, taking a collective deep breath, and being convinced that you can get through it all. Telling and hearing the stories of truth can generate within the congregation anxiety and fear. This strong emotional response must be managed, neither ignored nor squelched. Church officers will serve their weakening church well by first dealing with their own fears. The new pastor should be involved in this process, and it will take some time before enough trust is built to sustain the release of anxiety. Church officers then play a significant role in assuring the congregation, with its new pastor, that they will work together, learning what they need to learn, in order to lead the church.

These last matters begin to delve into topics for upcoming chapters, so we will take them up again later.

Don't leave the new pastor "hanging out to dry". Set up a way for your pastor to talk over his or her new pastoral experiences with designated board members. You do not want any landmines going off in the church because the pastor was too new to know what to expect. Your church benefits when its new pastor can discuss impressions and experiences among those charged with guiding your church. Officers who participate in these debriefings must be committed to the welfare of the church rather than to promoting one agenda or another.

Don't let the new pastor walk into potential crossfire between disagreeing church members. Many weakening congregations have endured a recent painful episode that fractured trust among members. It is tempting in the wake of such an episode for members on one side or another of the contest to want to win over their new pastor. Church members can succumb to temptations of power and deception. Tragically, these temptations seem to be fortified as a church declines. Ultimately, the authority for the church's welfare rests with its governing board. It will take courage to protect the pastor from fights that only symbolize the church's need for renewal. In many ways, courage is a spiritual quality. This is an important time in the church's life to discover such courage inside of yourselves, as you seek God's Spirit and guidance.

HOSPITALITY: A GIFT OF MYSTERY

Every time a congregation receives a new pastor, a mysterious and hopefully wonder-filled dance begins. It is an unchoreographed dance that occurs when a church takes seriously its role as a host, extending gestures of good will and welcome to the stranger who has come to guide the church in ministry. There is no formula that makes a successful adoption between the pastor-as-guest and the host congregation a sure thing. We do have access, however, to a frame of reference, a model for seeing what is at stake for any church when its new pastor arrives. This model suggests appropriate ways to move onto the dance floor, to take the hand of your new partner in ministry, and to discover how to glide across that floor together. As we have seen, both the guest and the host have roles to play, if the dance is to be worked out and performed. You are already at the party, as your new pastor walks in. How can your hospitality give him or her the chance to become the Fred Astaire to your Ginger Rogers?

❖ *five* ❖

CULTURAL CAPITAL

The Currency of Power

WHAT KIND OF POWER IS THIS?

At the beginning of this book, you read the story of Rev. Morgan's difficult resignation from his parish. It is a story of unresolved differences, incomplete conversations, hidden agendas, a conscientious but confused pastor, and a congregation left in the dark. This story is all these things—and more. We are speaking here about one of the least understood and most abused certainties in any church: that of power.

What do stories about unhappy pastoral partings reveal about the interaction of pastors and churches? From the church's standpoint, under what circumstances should pastors get their way? What is that delicate dance like between pastor and congregation, where decisions get made and actions result? Is a religious use of power truly possible?

In this chapter, we will probe the meaning of power. Our vantage point is the field of culture. There is a tremendous need for both clergy and church bodies to possess a clear-eyed view of what power is. Make no mistake: the notion of "power" is easily misconstrued. By reframing it here in terms of culture, we hope to demystify power. We can suspend judgment on its nature, what it can do, and of whether it can be used as part of our life of faith and witness. Power is a complex thing, but we can get a handle on it.

It might not occur to you that power actually exists in your congregation. This kind of power can also be called mana, an anthropological term describing power as it exists and functions within a community. This notion is parallel to the language of this book, as we speak here of cultural capital, key culture bearers, and dominant subcultures. Your congregation is encouraged to become aware of the particular ways that power functions within it. How does the mana, the cultural capital available within your congregation, help you "get along" in ministry? How do you share power with your pastor? These become central questions for a church that seeks to be both genuinely faithful and practically effective.

Our tasks, then, in finding our way through the sometimes intimidating halls of power are threefold. First, we will reflect on scripture, to get some idea of how power is both represented and interpreted. Secondly, we will frame power in cultural terms. Third, we will indicate some practical ways that the power of culture can be used faithfully.

BIBLICAL WITNESSES TO POWER

In their attempts to understand the Bible, Christians encounter an interesting irony concerning the realities of power. On the one hand, readers will find ample evidence of biblical characters who exercise power—who make things happen and who sometimes impose their way upon others. Ancient terms that are translated into the English word "power" comprise about 250 entries, in both the Hebrew Bible and the New Testament.[1] These references, of course, indicate only a fraction of the narratives and other biblical passages in which incidents of power can be observed.

Interpreting Jesus

What is not so apparent, however, is a clear interpretation of power itself in the Bible, one that can inform and guide Christian faith today. This confusion is evident even in references to Jesus. A common view of Jesus' crucifixion and resurrection suggests that human power is destructive (as symbolized by Roman execution) and must be overcome by God.

This apparent dichotomy between human power and God's power finds reinforcement, it seems, in the writings of Paul. The

Roman cross used to execute Jesus becomes a symbol of power, Paul claims (1 Cor. 1:17), although it appears as "foolishness" to those who have not received the good news (1 Cor. 1:18). God selected "what is weak in the world to shame the strong" (1 Cor. 1:27b), which for Paul becomes his model for ministry. Texts like these have had a deep effect on pious Christian efforts to understand the relationship between human living and God's ways. The two appear to be opposites of each other. A believer's exercise of power must be tainted by the wrong spirits, by a desire to be as gods (Gen. 3:1–5).

The Power of Human Action

Conclusions like these are hard to dispute when considering the frequency of biblical stories in which humans assert power for their own ends. Cain kills his brother Abel out of jealousy (Gen. 4:3–8); Jacob tricks Esau out of the latter's birthright (Gen. 25:29–34) and then seals it by stealing the blessing of inheritance from Isaac (Gen. 27). The favored warrior and king David arranges for Bathsheba's faithful husband to be abandoned during battle, thus assuring his death and David's eventual marriage to his pregnant lover (2 Sam. 11). Story lines like these cast a questionable light on the prudence of human agency. It easily could appear to a reader today that any effort on the part of a person of faith to get what they want is doomed. God's favor, by contrast, seems only for those who assert nothing but to follow God's will.

Complicating the negative view of human power are the biblical accounts of armed combat. Moses leads the Israelites at God's bidding to defeat kings Sihon and Og (Num. 21:21–35). Joshua continues the Israelite conquest, directed by God (see Josh. 10:40–43; 12). David's military accomplishments expanded Israel's geographic reach (2 Sam. 2, 8–10). War did not always favor God's chosen people, however. Theological interpretations throughout the Hebrew Bible indicate that war tended to favor Israel if they trusted God and went against Israel if they had turned away from God (see, for example, Ps. 106).

What kind of power does God intend for humans to use? For what purposes or ends? If God can use military force to "defeat the enemies of the chosen ones," where does that leave the use of power between the congregation and its pastor?

SORTING OUT OUR CONFUSION

We have only begun to think here about power as we find it exhibited in the Bible; but from even this brief treatment let's draw a few important conclusions. First, although biblical texts themselves provide very little direct instruction about power, a considerable amount of the Bible's narrative and other forms of content deals with power, its forms, and its uses. Second, we who read the Bible today interpret much of what we read based on assumptions that we bring to the text. Sometimes we read into stories, proverbs, and exhortations beliefs that not necessarily promoted by the text itself.

Third, it seems many well-meaning Christians believe that the only way in which power can be good is if it is God's. So how do we know when God's power is at work? Are we to yield all of our human potential for power, to behave as though we have none? Is this realistic? How would this view of power play itself out in our churches?

CLAIMING POWER

If we have this much trouble being clear about power in general, we should not be surprised that our churches sometimes have trouble working out power relationships with their pastors. Let us, then, identify one of the primary claims of this chapter—that *power is neutral.* We begin our exploration into congregational power with this assertion. By nature, power is neither good nor bad; it is what it is. If we assume instead, as many Christians have tended to do, that power is simply bad, we have a hard time dealing with the world in which we live. A more useful starting point is that there is nothing wrong with power in itself.

Second, what makes this claim about power tenable is its companion definition. Simply stated, *power is the ability to accomplish something, to make things happen.* This definition is broad, meaning that it covers a wide range of actual ways that power occurs. Power is manifested in many forms, in many kinds of locations, at various times—and all of these manifestations can and do shift, based on circumstances and possibilities. Not all power is exercised against the will of others. However, "against the will of others" is often the way that people think about power. In the church, force is not always a helpful way to frame power.

Third, *power is not confined to office and authority.* This is a point that I emphasize with seminary students. I explain to them that they indeed will fulfill a role in the office of pastor, which grants them certain designated, official authority. This authority, however, does not come with a license to be powerful, that is, for the pastor to do whatever the pastor wants. A cultural view of church life gives us a framework for understanding how power grows and shifts. Pastors have to become adopted by their church if they are to gain the power that cultural capital makes possible.

Finally, let us consider for our purposes here that *power includes the capacity for influencing the decisions and actions of others.* In many cases, this means that power occurs informally, rather than through the official actions of an officeholder. Consider Paul's letter to Philemon. The apostle never came right out and insisted that the slave owner release Onesimus back to Paul, even though he felt "bold enough in Christ" (v. 8) to do so. As one under house arrest, Paul had no resources at his disposal for using physical force to threaten Philemon. Yet, there is little doubt by the conclusion of the letter about what Paul expects Philemon to do. Paul employed the power of persuasion. He appealed to the common faith that master and slave now shared, to respect for Paul's age, to his condition of house arrest, and to the awareness that the congregation hosted by Philemon heard the request, too. You can say that Paul is pretty sly, but he does let Philemon make up his own mind.

As you think about these four basic claims concerning power, ask yourself a few questions:

- ❖ Which persons in your church are powerful because of the office they hold? Which ones are powerful because of other factors? What are some of those factors?

❖ What might be some of the submerged beliefs that exist in your church's cultural mud—about human nature, human activity, and human relationships—that are supporting the ways in which power is exercised?

CULTURE AS POWER

A pastor's ability to get something done or to make something happen depends in large part upon the congregation's acceptance, trust, and respect. As this acceptance is generated, the pastor in effect is being ushered into the world of that congregation's cultural capital. She or he gradually is able to do more and more, to be more powerful, by continuing to show genuine regard for aspects of the church's life that are considered fundamental. *You, as a member of the congregation, are much more likely to be in tune with what makes your church tick than is your new pastor.* You and other members probably cannot easily articulate "what makes your church tick," but you sense when it is being violated. You are intuitively aware of the presence of certain submerged beliefs in the church's cultural mud. Your pastor can either affirm or deny these submerged items by his or her behavior. What she or he says (sayings) and does (stuff) symbolizes support of the congregation.

When a new pastor in worship recognizes and praises the church "mother" or another respected church member, the congregation sees an act of honor for deep congregational values and practices. When a new pastor changes some of the chancel furniture without anyone else's knowledge, the congregation likely will get upset. Sanctuaries carry significant cultural symbolism and are not easily changed, especially for churches in decline. Church members rightfully become concerned when a pastor behaves this way!

Once you have initially adopted your pastor, how can you learn to share power with him or her? Here are a few general suggestions:

Identify the key elements of cultural power in your congregation. The most strategic place to begin this kind of learning is with your congregation's governing body. It needs to learn how to perceive the deeper meanings of everything that the church does and says. This means becoming adept at making connections and seeing contradictions between the cultural layers. Which of your cherished objects, rituals, and activities (stuff) are related to which of your submerged beliefs? Which of your sayings, as grand as they might sound, are supported or contradicted by one or more of your stuff? Don't be in a hurry to come up with answers. These are the deepest matters that affect your pastor's ability to serve with you.

Locate your congregation's current phase on the organizational lifecycle. In the Old Testament, one of the tasks of prophets was to tell the truth about God's people, even when they did not want to hear it or believe it. God's prophets are right, even when they are not popular. Your church has a chance to do its own prophetic work, as difficult as it might be. You are challenged and encouraged to pinpoint what the entire swamp analysis (all three layers) suggests about your lifecycle phase. Be honest! The majority of churches in the United States today are not up and coming or dynamic; instead, they have slipped into the established and even weakening phases.

Use the descriptions of the phases in chapter 2 to guide a serious, thoughtful conversation about lifecycle location. Remember that the purpose for these swamp and lifecycle analyses is to benefit your ministry. How does your current phase affect your pastor's ability to share in the congregation's power? What kind of cultural capital does the current condition of the church's culture allow the pastor to acquire and use?

Clarify your church's history of pastoral expectations, using insights from your two sets of analysis. Your culture is the result of what your church has learned together over the years. The identifiable things that your church hopes to receive from its pastor are based on its specific experiences and how those experiences formed relationships between stuff on your shore and submerged beliefs in your mud. By uncovering the specific stories that are tied to certain expectations, your congregation will learn more about itself. Then you will be in a better position to judge which expectations are now realistic and viable and which ones will not serve you well anymore. You want your pastor to be able to walk without running into landmines that you knew were there but could not help your pastor avoid.

THE POWER OF CULTURE—YOUR PASTOR AND YOU

Culture, then, is tightly intertwined with the power of any organization, even congregations. That is why we have introduced and applied the term "cultural capital" here. *Culture's power is real; it takes time to develop; it is invisible to outsiders; and it does not shift easily.* Furthermore, because culture is a phenomenon describing communities (that is, collections of persons rather than individuals), the power of culture is grounded in a particular community. Individual persons are able to exercise power on the basis of their relationship to that community. That relationship gets all tied up in culture as swamp, as lifecycle, and as confluence. The pastor who is ushered into the deeper life of a congregation, honoring and respecting what she or he finds, builds cultural capital in that church.

Let us now see how each phase of the cultural lifecycle affects the way that a church can share power with its pastor.

Up-and-Coming Phase

If your founding pastor is gone, which current members of the congregation are part of its founding network? I was working once with a congregation that was twenty-seven years old and going through some transitions. It had built a large, inviting sanctuary, a creatively designed fellowship hall, and a separate education facility. The previous pastor had just left under a cloud, however, and most of the members were not sure what had gone wrong. The church's governing board invited several key culture bearers to join it for a day of swamp analysis. This body then self-selected into three groups, based on being newcomers, longtime members, or those somewhere in between. First the entire group generated a list of church stuff and church sayings. These groups then spent some time among themselves with lists of stuff and sayings generated by the whole group in front of them.

Self-selected groups were asked to identify submerged beliefs. The in-between group reported one submerged belief to be, "The only people with real power in our church are the charter members." When their representative read this statement aloud, the charter members sitting with the longtime group appeared surprised and hurt. They replied that they always welcomed new members to participate.

This story illustrates how the power of a church's founding members can be subtle and hidden. This congregation appeared to be resourceful and fairly cooperative. Yet some members perceived a deep assumption in their church about power. The charter members were not aware of ways in which their words and deeds were interpreted as control. Still, the founding network—of whomever it consists—will influence the church significantly. Can you analyze their part in your young congregation, without judgment, yet with insight?

What is the congregation still negotiating, and whose voices are most able to get their way? During this first lifecycle phase, the congregation is still working out the various decisions regarding the four functions of envisioning, performing, relating, and executing (see chapter 2). Pay attention to how these decisions get made: that very process—including the key players—will create submerged beliefs, one way or another. A new pastor could be put in a position of having little voice, if you are not careful. Is this what you want your church to become? Or are you willing to develop ministry through conversation—even in the face of problems? This is the time when you want both the church's board and congregation to be learning that problems are normal. You can talk about them, you can learn from each other and as a group, and the pastor can take a productive role.

How robust have some of the church's practices and beliefs become? It is not too early for the church's governing board to begin learning how to pay attention to the church's cultural swamp. All of the congregation's three cultural layers are still developing. Take time to reflect on this formation. Begin asking yourselves "why" concerning any of the stuff on the shore that is becoming set in stone. Remember that nothing stays up on the shore without being connected to something down in the mud.

How influential is your pastor? Where would that cultural capital go if this particular pastor were not there anymore? Young organizations need guidance and support; when a trusted guide is gone, the organization is at risk. Whoever is granted this role will influence the church greatly. If you expect a new pastor to do this, you need to be a warm and honest host. Otherwise, a church member might decide that a void exists and try to fill it in inappropriate ways.

Dynamic Phase

Who has emerged as the congregation's heroes? The dynamic phase is not a time when pastors typically move, since they usually have been integral to the church's visible success. Hence, pastors in dynamic churches typically become part of the heroic stories that the congregation passes on. Cultural capital provides pastors in dynamic-phase churches with power to continue influencing the church's practices.

If the congregation loses a pastor while it is still dynamic, that pastor likely will become even more honored in the church's memory. This might make adoption of the next pastor more difficult, thus triggering the congregation's move into decline. Heroes help the congregation when they are utilized to keep the congregation fresh, open, and faithful—rather than nostalgic and wistful. You want all of your heroes' (dead or alive) power to stimulate the energy to keep your church dynamic.

What are the church's various subcultures? Is one of them beginning to dominate the others? Dynamic churches have to have some division of labor, simply to accomplish what they do well at this point. This branching off into more specialized activity is normal, and it creates subcultures with their own "miniswamps" inside the church's overall cultural swamp. Be careful, though; it is easier to identify the groups themselves than the subcultures that grow out of them. For instance, it is not just the music department as such that can become influential; rather, it is the submerged beliefs shared between their subculture and the church's culture that are the source of any music power.

A pastor who is perceived to be aligned with one subculture over others faces risks. One is limiting her or his access to cultural capital, the stuff of power, by alienating a different subgroup. Another is unwittingly setting up circumstances in the congregation that develop into conflict between groups. The pastor's job in the dynamic phase is to keep power flowing from the church's vision, not from special interests.

How are decisions made? How is the congregation's vision employed to guide decisions? In the dynamic phase, pastors do not make all the decisions; they are worked out through formal and informal processes within the church. Committees, auxiliaries, and key culture bearers all contribute. It will be important to your new pastor to be ushered into this process, rather than left to figure it out hit or miss.

Strong vision that is clear, articulated, and compelling makes it possible for the church's power to be focused and utilized in the right way. Vision is always bigger than any one person or group within the congregation. When utilized, vision makes the pastor's job one of the eagle and the sage. The eagle function is the pastor's responsibility to help the church's governing board maintain the big picture of the congregation's life and work. The sage function is the pastor's responsibility to provide the board and church with the kind of wisdom that helps them make good decisions. You want your pastor to help you remain accountable to the vision itself.

Established Phase

Who are recognized as the "power people" in your congregation? How do they use their influence? As decline begins, one of the dangers to the congregation is that power begins to become concentrated. It is natural for key culture bearers to exist and be active in this phase. What will hurt the congregation, especially in the long run, is if these culture bearers use the power of their cultural capital to promote a narrowing agenda. Your pastor's challenge is to gain enough trust and respect with these persons to be able to keep them looking at the church as a whole and at its future. This is the best time for a congregation to recover from its subtle slip into organizational decline. Ultimately, this recovery is your pastor's primary task, and the key culture bearers must participate.

How is the congregation's energy turning increasingly into itself? Established organizations become less attentive to what occurs around them (changes in cultural confluence) and increasingly preoccupied with their own matters. As a result, the power of the culture becomes devoted primarily to maintaining the organization's status quo. Again, one of the central strategic issues for your church is to learn to keep analyzing itself. Its tendency will be exactly the opposite—to ride the wave of achievement from its recent past. It takes energy to persuade your church's governing board to lead the church by looking in the mirror. Otherwise, power patterns become very predictable, and your pastor could become hindered in acquiring cultural capital.

Weakening Phase

What kind of disagreements or conflicts has the congregation experienced in the last few years? How do key culture bearers use their power? What place is the pastor granted? The church's decline now is taking a visible toll. Even the key culture bearers cannot prevent disagreements from touching the congregation's public arena. Longtime members do not trust each other as much as they used to. As you think about a new pastor, your life together will be better off if you can find a way to accept that struggles have hurt you. Weakening churches are usually embarrassed or unresolved about their internal contests; they want to hide these from their pastor. Ironically, however, this tactic backfires: the pastor ends up running into the cultural residue of the troubles anyway. Often this makes the pastor look bad, so the church has someone else to blame, but with no long-term benefits. *Pastors serving weakening churches need to develop the cultural capital necessary to help the church use its power in new ways.* If your church understands this, it can intentionally foster adoption as a necessary step toward new life.

What does the congregation say that it wants from its pastor? What happens when the pastor actually does these things? To what submerged beliefs in the mud are these "sayings" connected? Weakening churches have not figured out how to get out of their downward spiral, so they imagine that the new pastor can do it for them. They often will make sincere statements about their intentions. "We want to grow"; "we want families with young children"; "we are warm and friendly to visitors."

Danger! Weakening churches experience the greatest contradiction of any phase between what they say and what they do.

I once served a small, older congregation that said it wanted to attract more families. As I reached out to young couples and encouraged them to participate in the life of this church, I realized that the church said one thing but meant something else. The dominant subculture was not interested in new members unless they fit right into what already was happening and helped support the budget as it was. The new members were discovering that they were not very welcome. The congregation's overall behavior contradicted its saying.

Unless the weakening church commits itself to change and works toward change while it deals with its anxieties, it never will grant its pastor any power. The best that a pastor could do under these circumstances is to function as a chaplain—someone who supports the members through their life joys and trials. This function certainly will strengthen the pastor's cultural capital in the congregation. What it will not do, however, is position the church to partner with its pastor for "a new thing."

How much is publicly discussed about the congregation's current situation? By the time a congregation has moved into the weakening phase, all the longtime members know that something is wrong. Until there is a conversation about it, however, this church cannot release the energy that has gone dormant within itself. Too often, these conversations occur privately, laced with fear about the future. The power needed to move the church into a process of new vitality can be stimulated *only as the church first tells the truth about itself and then is led by a small group committed to change.*[2] If your pastor is to be a key to this process, she or he needs to have built up power through the cultural capital that already exists in the church.

CONCLUSION: POWER CONSCIOUS, NOT POWER HUNGRY

Rev. Morgan's reluctant resignation, in the story from the introduction, was triggered by an angry board member's abrupt demand. Rather than follow this congregation's bylaws, this board member bypassed the opportunity to air her grievances in an open process. Joyce was a key culture bearer in her church, and she used her own cultural capital to undermine that of her church's new pastor.

Fear can generate the use of forceful power, often in destructive ways. Rev. Morgan's experience is nothing if not a rude reminder of our human condition, subject to our sinfulness and its consequences. None of us is exempt from temptation to use power to serve our own purposes, even if that pursuit works against the will of others.

Congregations are communities of faith, saved by grace, depending upon the Holy Spirit to live out of that grace. In such a theological context, there is nothing wrong with power. It will and does exist in our churches. What we have sought in this chapter is a way to see how power actually functions. With these cultural lenses, we can describe the subtleties of power around the theme of cultural capital. You don't need to try to reject it, to pretend that it is not there, to run it out of camp on a scapegoat. Instead, you can work with this power to help your church deal with its normal problems of change, of fear, and of tension. You can become skilled at drawing in your pastor to the power of your church's culture, because she or he cannot help you otherwise.

To acknowledge the reality of power, as well as of our human frailties, means that we inevitably face the prospect of conflict, even within our churches. Yet even the sting of dissension can inflict much less harm than we might suppose. To see how, let us turn to the next chapter.

✤ *six* ✤

CONFLICT, THE CRUCIBLE

Becoming Peacemakers in a Mean World

NOT A PRETTY PICTURE

Do you really want me to try to tell you how bad church conflict is getting these days? I could tell you many stories:

- The young, talented, and earnest choir director who re-signed after a misstep in trying to establish more discipline during rehearsals
- The church trustee who cursed me for inviting an engineer to look at the church building without permission from the board of trustees
- Pastors who change the arrangement of sanctuary furniture without permission, change the music in morning worship without warning, hire a new staff member without using the proper procedure
- Two or three active members who take their disagreements over a particular church activity into the congregation's public life

I could give you a long list of books and other resources prepared by consultants, church officials, and others, designed to help churches work through their conflicts constructively.[1]

Yes, church conflict has become an epidemic. It is a killer—and a not-so-quiet one at that—of big dreams, for pastors and congregations alike. Conflict in congregations has become so prevalent that some of the people and organizations just referred to are table-talk conversation when church folks get together.

At the beginning of each semester, students in my classes usually write a three-page paper about "a church episode or issue" in which they participated. I deliberately do not refer to conflict or disagreement when I explain the paper's range of possible topics. What happens every semester, however, is that about one-half of the students write directly of conflicted situations.

To what extent are today's churches and other religious groups going through serious discord? What happens to pastors, associates, music ministers, youth directors, and church members when the conflict results in people leaving? What happens to their faith and desire to witness to the gospel? These are questions that I have asked myself for years. More recently, however, I have come to ask myself another question: *when disputes run their course, what happens to the congregation?*

THE CULTURE OF CONFLICT

Culture plays a central part in organizational conflict, even that of a church's. The ways in which the members of an organization perceive culture while working through organizational stress, anxiety, and contests lead to creation of certain submerged beliefs in the organization's cultural mud. In many cases, the congregation comes to believe deep down that controversies are too hard to handle, that a few people end up "getting their way," that new ideas pose threats to what the church most cherishes. Then, when the dust finally settles, something else has happened as well. The church has lost an opportunity to discover whether its calling as a community of faith leads it to pursue something new.

In this chapter, therefore, we construe the phenomenon of conflict differently. We frame it as a crucible, a testing ground, a *kairos* moment. As a phenomenon of your congregation's culture, dissension symbolizes more than what you think it does. The previous two chapters, on pastoral adoption and church power, touched often on the theme of conflict. Here, our reframing of conflict culturally provides the basis for learning how to use discord to the church's benefit.

Why is it important for a congregation to learn how to work through its arguments? For the purposes of this book, the answer should be self-evident: so you can get along with your pastor. I do not mean merely accommodating a difficult person or circumstances, just to get by. Rather, "getting along with your pastor" sets the stage for your church's Christian witness. Conflict points to this stage in its most dramatic terms.

We have two basic tasks in this chapter, then. The first is to analyze church conflict through a cultural lens. What we discover is that the perceived issue is never the real issue. Instead, what is fundamentally at stake are particular contents in your church's cultural mud. Differences in valuing submerged beliefs do pop up between church members or groups of members. The pastor's place in the discord is a function of how the congregation perceives him or her behaving in the midst of it. The second task is to discuss the implications of cultural analysis for how a church can work through its own disputes. There is a better way!

How, then, can your congregation learn how to get along with your pastor in such a way that

♦ the congregations knows how to work through its own disagreements (typical ones and otherwise) without wounding people;

♦ the pastoral office in your church maintains the honor that it needs to serve you well; and

♦ your community comes to see your church as a place where peace is made?

CONFLICT AND LIFECYCLE

Let us be clear: dissension is more likely in certain phases of the lifecycle than in others. Surely disagreements can arise any time in a congregation's life, but how they are perceived and handled can and does vary dramatically. Many episodes of church discord begin with an incident that, in itself, does not necessarily have to trigger lots of quarreling. *The rule of thumb in lifecycle terms is that you can expect conflict more frequently—and pos-*

sibly more intensely—at either end of the lifecycle and less in the middle. Why is this the case?

To understand this rule of thumb, recall some of the features of lifecycle and cultural development. In the congregation's earliest years, culture is being created. Submerged beliefs take their place in the young church's mud as the members test out all the sayings and behaviors of the founding cadre (mainly the pastor and key charter members). The founding pastor's own cultural assumptions are put to the test. Many, if not most, of the differences of opinion that emerge in the *up-and-coming* phase revolve around whether the pastor's cultural baggage is workable and trustworthy for the infant church.

Potential disagreement is an occupational hazard for up-and-coming churches, so learning how to respond to such incidents when they arise becomes a critical goal.

On the other side of the lifecycle curve, *weakening* churches have lost strength because of their ongoing lack of response to change occurring around them. Thus, while the up-and-coming church is still negotiating its cultural swamp, the weakening church has been protecting its swamp. That is, it has maintained its stuff, its sayings and its submerged beliefs as inherited from an earlier, more vibrant era. As we have seen already, the submerged beliefs in this phase represent primarily what worked for the church in its early years, not what will work for it now. Submerged beliefs can appear solid, but in the weakening phase, many of them actually are rather rigid and frail.

Since longtime members intuitively realize that the *submerged beliefs* of their weakening church are indeed fragile, they experience high anxiety if they perceive those beliefs to be threatened. All it takes is for something new to appear or be proposed among the church's (long-established and now aging) *stuff*. It could be all kinds of things—unfamiliar hymns in worship, a change in liturgy, replacement of cherished objects of remembrance (for example, a chair in the chancel or the parlor), visitors who look and behave differently than the congregation, a proposal to merge with another church, and the like. Most new things (stuff) in a weakening congregation will not be connected to anything in the church's cultural mud (submerged beliefs). Even proposing a new saying (perhaps "a church that cares for its community") could trigger dissent from the dominant subculture.

DIAGRAM J—What Are the Connections in Your Church between Layers of Culture?

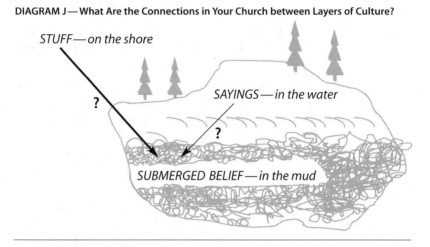

Weakening churches and up-and-coming churches both are at risk for conflict. In times of discord, what kind of challenges does a congregation in one of the at-risk zones face with its pastor? The tendency in most disagreements, as we know, is for the situation to be framed as either-or: either the pastor gets what the pastor wants, or the members or a cluster of members get what they want. When the contest is viewed as between two groups of members, the pastor has to walk a fine line. Any difference of opinion in a congregation will draw in the pastor as a key player, at some point, in some way.

Discord affects a church's cultural mud differently, depending on its lifecycle phase. Young congregations are still "under cultural construction." Response to crisis shapes submerged beliefs that end up in its tender mud. If the members and pastor endure a strenuous episode of disagreement, filled with rancor, secret conversations, public accusations, and the like, the church's mud will suffer. That is, the congregation will learn things that will make it harder to get through the next quarrel. This is such an important point for new churches to understand. *The manner in which up-and-coming congregations treat their own internal discord creates cultural patterns that will reverberate into its future.* If young churches could commit themselves early on to seek peace in all that they do, they would learn valuable lessons for keeping themselves both faithful to the gospel and strong in witness.

Weakening congregations face a different kind of opportunity. Dissensions in its midst threaten to tear away at its chances for renewing its life. Because all of its stuff—facilities, sanctuary, order of worship, surviving programs and events—have been around a long time, they are cherished. This is because they all are mysteriously connected with submerged beliefs down in the mud. The connections themselves are not obvious to outsiders nor easily articulated by longtime members. When the stuff is so protected, anything that is perceived to compete with, change, or remove that stuff will lead to an anxious reaction by longtime members. If we attribute this anxiety to an internal psychological feature of the individual, we misunderstand its origin.

In other words, conflicts in weakening churches appear to threaten the very symbols of life to which the congregation clings. A pastor who seems to disregard these valued items and rituals is in danger of stimulating a conflict. The pastor might not even realize that she or he is getting ready to step on a "landmine." The pastor could be confused by what she or he first heard articulated compared with what she or he is now observing.

DIAGRAM K—Do You Really Mean What You Say in Your Church?

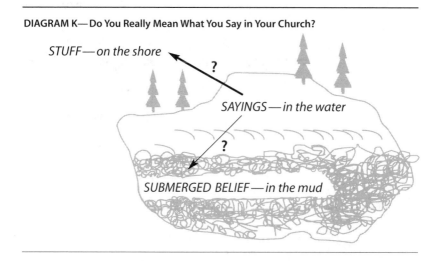

STUFF—on the shore

?

SAYINGS—in the water

?

SUBMERGED BELIEF—in the mud

These observations remind us again that getting along depends upon fostering a relationship that is sensitive to the cultural dynamics of both church and pastor. Weakening churches tend to assume that their pastors should fit right in and not do anything that the church does not want. It is no wonder, then, that so many pastors arrive at weakening churches eager to serve, but end up leaving unhappy. If the congregation does not realize this danger to their pastoral relationship, they are setting up their pastor for conflict and failure.

CONFLICT AND THE SWAMP

Our discussion of the lifecycle's effects upon the potential for congregational conflict has utilized the swamp metaphor as well. This is because the lifecycle phases reveal ways in which the swamp takes shape, stabilizes, and then becomes inflexible over the lifecycle. In this section, we are considering scenarios in the swamp that are *more likely to occur in the dynamic and established phases,* when the swamp is stable and has not yet become too rigid. Discord can arise between church groups whose histories have created subcultures; the respective submerged beliefs of one group will not overlap entirely with those of other

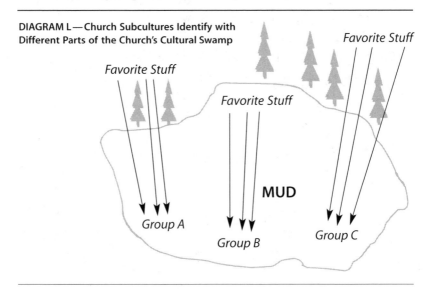

DIAGRAM L—Church Subcultures Identify with Different Parts of the Church's Cultural Swamp

groups. These subcultures in churches are often represented by particular committees and departments such as music ministry, facilities operation, education, local mission, international mission, and so on.

Over time, subgroups in churches get more focused on their specific part of the church's life and tend to lose the big picture. Discord in churches under these circumstances often emerges as a contest between the interests of two of these groups, say, the youth ministry and the music ministry (perhaps over the nature of a special program), or the trustees and the women's auxiliary (possibly regarding who has possession of keys to the parlor). What makes these forms of quarreling distinct is that the pastor might not have anything to do with the clash's origin. How the pastor responds to finding out about the trouble affects not only the outcome but the pastor's cultural capital.

This form of potentially escalating dispute therefore is somewhat different than what typically happens in the early and late phases. There, the pastor easily can be "in on the ground floor" of emerging discord. Whether he is at ground zero or on the fringes, at some point it will not matter. *If you want your pastor to lead, you must avoid scapegoating your pastor when tension mounts.* Even when you are convinced that the pastor has made things worse, a cultural framework informs you that there is more at stake for your church than you realize.

CONFLICT AND CONFLUENCE

Church disputes are also affected by streams of culture—although church members usually do not recognize this factor. Confluence theory claims that flowing waters of culture originate from a number of varying sources outside of the congregation. Our immediate experience in church is deeply yet subtlety affected by cultural elements that come from wider American society. Think of 1969, when baby boomers were coming of age and leading resistance to U.S. military action in Vietnam. Reflect on the reaction by many European American churches to the presence of people of color in worship, as members, and as fully active participants of the church's life. Consider what a retirement-age member of your church might think if a teenage girl today attends worship wearing low-rider jeans and a skimpy top. Imagine the conversations at an African American church when young adults argue for including hip-hop music during Sunday worship. Remember when women wore hats to church (in some churches, women still do!)? All these examples represent changes that have been taking place in recent years, originating in streams of culture outside of our churches. Some of the changes were macro-, that is, large-scale in effect. Others are meso-, linked to middle-level streams, having to do with race, gender, generations, and so on.

DIAGRAM M — How Many Streams of Culture Exist in Your Church?
How Open Are Your Members to Other Streams?

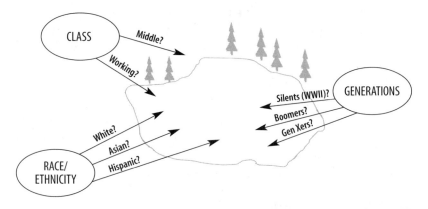

Confluence theory helps us appreciate how intricate is the world in which our churches function. Once you have a good idea of the confluence around your church, the next step is to ask: *Are these various streams creating smooth sailing or cultural logjams?* Sometimes your church does not even realize that its dispute is really over *what kind of cultural stuff, from which streams beyond your church, will be permitted.* New stuff symbolizes the possibility of new things down in the mud. Church conflict might be acted out over contents of the swamp without even acknowledging that the sources of those contents come from outside the church.

Your pastor can become an unwitting partner in dissension, based on how he or she pays attention to cultural confluence. Will your new pastor take sides with the youth (types of activities), or the trustees (use of property), or the music department (styles) on issues of change that originate in the world around you? Don't allow your pastor to be caught in one of those cultural logjams; they can be just as harmful as landmines!

To summarize, conflict potentials look a distinctive way when we consider the cultural elements involved. Far too often, the details, personalities, and behaviors that result from disputes overwhelm a church. Because church clashes with the pastor in the middle of it all hurt the church, your congregation has a vested interest in resolving differences more productively. What can a cultural approach to church conflict do to transform the way that a church conducts its affairs?

A MORE EXCELLENT WAY: CULTURAL JUJITSU

Many Americans are fascinated with the martial arts. The television series *Kung Fu,* the visually stunning motion picture *Crouching Tiger, Hidden Dragon,* the Bruce Lee movies—all these illustrate that Americans find something about Asian hand-to-hand combat techniques intriguing. At the heart of martial arts, however, is a worldview that differs from that of the modern West. This worldview is based in a set of submerged beliefs in Asian societies. In Asian philosophies what often appear to be opposites actually are complementary to each other. Energy exists both externally, in what it accomplishes visibly, and internally, invisible yet potent. In the martial arts, the master is one who has learned how to sense the energy present and to use it for his or her purposes. Instead of "fight the forces coming at you," martial arts is more like, "go with the energy that is there." How else can the master break bricks with one hand or throw someone much larger in size?

This chapter is urging your church to learn to "go with the energy." Looking at discord and potential conflict in a different way is like a form of cultural jujitsu. Typically, Americans respond to the perception of threat by trying to overcome its perceived source. A cultural framing of potential conflict begins by recognizing that energy is flowing. Instead of turning the situation into an either-or clash, a cultural-savvy church stays focused on its purpose in allowing energy to be used. *A cultural-savvy church learns how to direct energy,* to turn it toward useful ends.

This section, then, demonstrates how a church can use cultural jujitsu to redirect the energy of conflict. You cannot rely on your pastor to do it alone or to do it for you.

Theology and Conflict

A cultural approach to church life locates theology floating in the water of your church's cultural swamp. It is not embedded down in the mud. Theology thus is linked to the congregation's vision of God's purposes. In this way, theology is more about *hope—the way that things should be—*than it is about *reality— the way things are now.* The key question, then, is whether a church's theology is tested and found reliable, just like any other sayings would be tested.

Theology can take an active role in working through a congregation's dissension. Once the tension has been suspended sufficiently for key parties to talk, those parties pinpoint faith-based statements that are appropriate to affirm. They might sound something like one of these:

"Working together helps fulfill our calling as the body of Christ" (1 Cor. 12:12–27) Such an affirmation would serve to motivate everyone involved to focus on the congregation as a whole, rather than simply upon individual or subgroup interests. It also would affirm that the entire group benefits from the contributions of everyone.

"God will find a way out of no way."[2] Several biblical stories emphasize how the people of God faced what appeared to be insurmountable challenges but overcame them by trusting in God (for example, Abraham and Sarah as descendants for the promise, and the Israelites escaping from Egypt). A church in distress must believe that it can work through its wranglings, even when there might seem to be only impasse.

"We can make a difference in our world."[3] Churches who affirm that they can take action to deal with circumstances that

they face are more likely to handle conflict with less anxiety. Churches who feel helpless before the forces of their community and environment will tend to turn inward and fight among themselves, often destructively.

Beyond "The Issue"

A cultural interpretation of conflict also modifies a church's behavior through awareness. Rather than becoming obsessed with "fixing the problem," the church begins a decision-making process by reexamining itself. Specifically, the congregation steps back and reviews its culture. This process will uncover submerged beliefs in the congregation's cultural mud and bring to light any differences between church subcultures. Key culture bearers, who know the submerged beliefs "in their bones," benefit from hearing them articulated and discussing them with newer members. If your pastor is new, it offers her or him a wonderful opportunity to "fast-track" learning the cultural swamp. With these discoveries, those charged with overseeing the dispute can help everyone understand the situation more clearly. The question boils down to "What are the submerged beliefs at stake?"

Conflict and Cultural Capital

Cultural capital is not an official medium of exchange. It does not come automatically with church membership or with being hired, called, or appointed to the congregation. Pastors begin their ministry at a given church with very little cultural capital. In spite of its unofficial status, however, *cultural capital is real, pervasive, and very potent. It takes time to acquire,* and no one can use a calendar to determine whether he or she has been around long enough to gain sufficient amounts of it. Pastors come into most church situations at a disadvantage; the cultural capital almost entirely rests among the membership, particularly certain key members. These key culture bearers gained their cultural capital through years of participation and loyalty. It is not uncommon for key culture bearers to believe deep down that they know what is best for the church.

It is not surprising, then, that key culture bearers often end up in the middle of a church fracas. In some ways they have the most to lose. Pastors have to learn who these bearers are and which subcultures they represent. Your pastor needs a chance to play the kind of role in conflict that we hope pastors will play—as one who shows the congregation how to be peacemakers. He or she can help you use the church's cultural capital to test out your church's most cherished theological bearings. Theological reflection is an authentic form of Christian cultural jujitsu.

This jujitsu can work the other way, too. There might be times, especially in a pastor's early days with a new congregation, when she or he "steps on a landmine," blunders into something and didn't see it coming—or worse yet, did not care if the act set off a landmine. The church benefits in helping your new pastor recover from such a mistake. Conversations about the contents of the church's swamp will help to orient your pastor to its folkways. This means that your pastor will have a chance to become trusted and respected enough to help lead your church.

THE CULTURE OF CONFLICT: BECOMING MAKERS OF PEACE

By now, you realize that this chapter contains no secret formulae, no magic incantations, no simple dance-step method for dealing with conflict. You will not find old models from business, interpersonal relations, or even family systems in these pages. The textured life of congregations is too rich not to be explained culturally. What might seem to you to be a straightforward arrangement between pastor and church actually involves many elements that are subtle and intricate. The same is true for any disputes that might arise in your congregation. By reframing culturally, some of your concerns could be eliminated and others can be framed differently.

What you find in this chapter, then, are resources for interpreting what is really going on when dissension first appears. One of the first lessons to learn is that *the dynamics that generate differences of opinion are not bad in themselves*. It would be unrealistic to assume that congregations who aspire to be full of faith will never be at odds among themselves. Problems do not necessarily turn into conflict, and conflict does not necessarily hurt the church.

This discussion has been guided by a few main premises. One is that *contests in churches are not always as they appear.* The situation allows opportunity for the congregation to work on its deeper learning. The second premise is that *the better the church gets at seeing all three forms of culture at play, the more capable it is of diverting its energy away from a fight.* Third, *the insights and skills that the congregation can learn by handling dissension noncombatively actually strengthen it.* Church members can back away from frustration and anger; staff and board members learn together about the cultural forces that undergird their church's logjam; everyone is able to speak together and figure out a solution; people do not leave hurt and angry. Fourth, a cultural framework gives your church tools to link up with your biblical and theological values. Every church says that it is "warm and friendly"! What makes the lived-out difference? Culture tools equip you to see how to connect your religious sayings to your church's cultural foundations.

What would you rather your church learn to do—resolve its conflict, or keep itself strong and vital? What you are reading here seeks to help take your church beyond mere resolution. When Jesus spoke of peacemakers as those "called children of God" (Matt. 5:9), he was not making a trite comment. How many of our congregations give up a chance to be peacemakers by the way that they slug things out in a dispute? A larger opportunity is at stake every time you face differences of opinion. How can you use this tension-filled time to discover what peacemaking looks and feels like? This is one of the most profound challenges to any community of faith in the world today.

And where is the pastor in all this? Usually, she or he is right in the thick of things, one way or another. The person filling that role in your congregation symbolizes all of the threats and opportunities hidden in your church's mud. By isolating the pastor from the whole picture, you misread the situation, you hurt the pastor, and you end up hurting your church. Look beyond what seems obvious, attend to the clues about connections from sayings and stuff that reach down into the mud. Then, armed with some healthy detachment, both you and your pastor can figure out what course will serve your church's best ministry purposes.

This introduction to a cultural interpretation of pastor-church relationships is almost complete. We have not yet discussed the most important subject, however—leadership. Talking about leadership is not as simple as you might suppose. Prepare yourself, then, to see leadership differently. If you do, you will realize that we will be talking not only about your pastor. We will be talking about your church.

seven

SHARING LEADERSHIP

Vision, Challenge, Excitement

THE BIG PICTURE

Now it is time to see how all of this talk about culture, adoption, power, and conflict prepares your pastor to do what she or he is called to do: lead your congregation. Keep in mind: *the ultimate purpose for pastor and congregation getting along is to strengthen your church's gospel witness.* This is a goal that never should be forgotten, by either your church or your pastor.

Leadership is a topic that is discussed in many circles, is studied by historians and organizational theorists, is bandied about by media wags, and certainly grabs the attention in many church conversations. What is leadership? Do we know it when we see it? How is church leadership any different? What should leadership help churches accomplish?

Let us move beyond assumptions about leadership that often are left unexamined. Instead, let us be clearer about what leadership is—and what it is not.

A PROCESS OF ELIMINATION

To begin, we will narrow the field. There are a number of qualities or behaviors that we uncritically sometimes associate with leadership. By pointing out these specific characteristics, and explaining why they do not fill the bill, we can focus more readily upon what we seek to understand. Leadership is too important a need, in today's world, for us to think of it as one thing when it is something else.

Not This, Not That

For instance, *leadership is not to be equated with force.* Force is a form of power, but only one form. Spanking, jet rockets, hurricanes, home runs, terrorist attacks, war, and so forth all illustrate ways in which power as force can exhibit itself. Human force is often viewed as destructive or punitive, to hurt or to punish people; history and our own personal experiences provide ample evidence of this! Because force often does mean that some are imposing their will on others, we recognize its potential for being harmful. For this reason alone, it is not accurate to think of leadership simply in terms of force.

Similarly, *leadership is not to be associated with manipulation.* Sometimes people use others to get what they want. This also happens in churches. In certain situations, pastors might be tempted to use a doctrinal position or a religious tradition to control the behavior of church members. Such a tactic creates for that congregation a submerged belief about human relationships that I consider to be limiting rather than expansive. Manipulation can be powerful, but not all power leads.

Neither can acts of deception be considered leadership. One of my seminary students told the story in class of her pastor initiating a fund drive for the purpose, he stated, of constructing a family life center on the congregation's property. Church members gave sacrificially to the fund. Time passed, and the congregation waited. After eight years, the subject of the project came up at a church board meeting. The pastor would not say how much money was in the construction account, but he did admit that some of that money had been used to renovate and redecorate the sanctuary. With tears welling in the pastor's eyes, the board decided that their questions had been answered adequately. Was this pastor deceiving his congregation? The rest of the students in class that day thought so! Deception is a form of misleading, not leading.

Leadership also should not be confused with being busy or doing things for others. Some pastors are prone to being workaholics, not slowing down, not resting, always on the go. We also know that pastors can be tempted to suppose that "fixing" the problems of other people is their primary task. Helping others with needs certainly fulfills part of our Christian calling, but acts of service in themselves do not necessarily indicate leadership.

Furthermore, *leadership does not emerge automatically as the privilege of office.* Your city councilwoman, your state representative, your governor, your pastor, your school board president: are they leaders? It all depends. Holding an office certainly provides a person with the possibility of leading, since she or he is in a position to help make things happen. Yet, mere activity by virtue of office is not automatically leadership.

Holding office also reminds us that *leading is not about self-serving activity.* Stories appear all too frequently about elected officials who use their office for political and economic gain. Some of their actions seem downright brazen, as though the person believes that feathering his or her own nest comes as a "perk" of the office. In a nation that espouses democracy, free association, free speech, and open governmental proceedings, genuine leadership will look and act differently than it did many centuries ago. Self-service, privilege, deception, manipulation, and force work against what leadership in a democratic society needs to look like.

A Mixed Testimony

Pious readers of scripture often blush and stammer when encountering famous "biblical leaders" behaving badly. Deception, self-service, and all other forms of bad behavior appear among famous leaders in the pages of the holy writ in ample volume. Moses complained about his role as God's chosen leader for Israel's deliverance from Egypt (Exod. 3:11, 4:13). He got mad at the people more than once during their wilderness wanderings (Exod. 32:15–20, Num. 20:1–12). Yet, he is remembered as one of the Bible's great figures (Deut. 34:10–12).

King David's record as a divinely appointed leader is no less mixed. He was wildly popular as a military hero before he ascended the throne. His popularity continued, even after impregnating an army officer's wife and then arranging for the officer, Uriah, to be killed in battle (2 Sam. 11) so that he could marry the woman, Bathsheba. In these acts David was serving himself, not his subjects and not his nation.

Not Stuck

David's story also points out another thing that leadership is not. *Leadership is not permanent.* Praise and attention does not in itself indicate that the person is leading still. In spite of his expansion and uniting of the kingdom, and even in spite of his ancestral link to the birth of Jesus (see, for instance, Luke 2:4–11 and Matt. 1:4–6), David never led again after the Bathsheba incident. His distinctive place in biblical history should not cloud our understanding of David as a leader. When we assume that "once a leader, always a leader," we risk misplacing the community's energy for being led. Those who have led can lead again, but not merely because they did it once before.

Becoming aware that leadership is not limited to those who already have led suggests one more point about what leadership is not. Leadership is not exercised in only one way. *There is no one method or manner of leading.* Leadership and power are not identical, even when they work together. The traditional ways in which government, military, and business have undertaken their activities often leave the public believing that the only way to lead is to be aggressive. Let us be clear, however: leading is not confined to conventional, recognized practices of overcoming the will of another party. This point is especially significant for religious groups such as churches.

It was in a similar spirit that Robert Greenleaf, toward the end of his long business career with AT&T, began gathering his thoughts about large organizations and speaking and writing about them. Greenleaf's essays promote the notion of "servant leadership." In history, it is much more common to see an "abnormal and corrupting" form of authority, in which the "lone chief" sits at the top of a structural pyramid. Greenleaf argues that the person in the top position has access to too much power, which inevitably creates more concern to regulate than to lead.

Instead, servant leadership shifts to a structure of authority in which the organization operates with a "first among equals," in which obligation and responsibility are shared.[1] Greenleaf is arguing for a form of leading that occurs by using power differently than by force.

LEADERSHIP IN A NUTSHELL

Greenleaf's proposal turns our discussion away from saying what leadership is not and toward what leadership actually is. As a subject, leadership increasingly garners attention from researchers and writers in many fields.[2] Many of these leadership studies do not approach the topic as comprehensively as does the culture model in this book. Churches and pastors benefit from recognizing and working with the complex factors that make leadership possible. These all center around the role of vision.

Centrality of Vision

Leading requires vision. What exactly is vision, though? How does it relate with mission? How and why is vision at the center of leading?

What makes vision distinct is its overarching perspective. Henry Ford's vision was of every American family with an affordable means of transportation. Those who helped to establish the United States of America pursued a vision of an independent union of states operating by the principles of representative democracy. *Vision consists of a picture of the future, an appealing sketch of something better that has not yet come into being.* For a community of faith to follow vision, it must discern God's call in its particular setting and circumstances. As mission, goals, strategies, and details become implemented, vision comes closer to being fulfilled. Vision remains the reference point for all of the church's activities.

Vision, then, grounds any form of leadership. Because vision is any organization's most deep-seated need, those who guide the group to fulfill its vision are leading. Many people still assume that leadership centers on what one person accomplishes. This popular view misses two points. The first is that, in the end, what matters is the group's accomplishment (there are no leaders without followers). The second is that not every accomplishment expresses the fulfillment of a vision. If we lose the forest for the trees, we have no vision, and therefore we have no leadership.

CULTURAL INTERPRETATION

So, then, *to lead is to help a community articulate an exciting possible future and to pursue that future as the purpose of its existence.* If the vision indeed is about creating a world that is not yet as it could be, things will not stay exactly the same. Recognizing the reality of change, therefore, is another basic element in leading.

Experience with change can be guided fruitfully by insights from culture theory. First, vision itself has a different role at different lifecycle phases. Second, a church's cultural swamp contains different things in the mud in different phases of the lifecycle. Third, change is influenced by the cultural streams in the church's surroundings. Let us briefly explore each of the culture theories for clues to leading.

Leading in the Lifecycle

Issues involving vision and change do not stay the same from one lifecycle phase to another.

Up-and-coming In this phase, leading tends to be centered in personality. For churches, this usually means the personalities of the founding pastor and/or one or two others. This small cadre is most influential in all of the key decisions. Vision is interpreted and articulated by that pastor, whose charisma provides virtually all the initial driving energy.

Over time, however, that vision and energy need to shift. *The vision will have to take on a life of its own, not tied so closely to the founder.* That person or persons must prove their will and discipline to change modus operandi for the benefit of the organization. This challenge is not simple or easy, but make no mistake: this is the eventual challenge to her or his capacity for leading.

If your church is still in the up-and-coming phase, ask yourself the following questions:

- ❖ Does your pastor have the inner strength and insight to "allow the baby to walk on its own"?
- ❖ Who has the pastor's respect enough to help the pastor understand the transition that both pastor and congregation eventually face?
- ❖ Can the church accept this shift without fear or blaming?

Dynamic In the dynamic phase, things are going so well that the organization almost feels like it could run by itself. Activities focus on excellent results, leaving organizational members and staff almost giddy with accomplishment. The danger is that the church will get stuck in ruts of its own making, convinced that its past successes will determine its ongoing achievement.

At some point, the dynamic congregation's vision needs to be revisited, in light of the congregation's self-awareness and its community. How often? As often as change around the church occurs. *To lead in the dynamic phase, then, means to keep an eye on the vision as well as on signs of change.* Leadership—including evaluation processes and disciplines of conversation—is best shared, by the pastor, the staff, and the governing board.

- ❖ How clear, how articulated and how compelling is its vision? Be honest now!
- ❖ When was the last time that the church tried something new?
- ❖ What do the pastor and governing board discuss on a regular basis?
- ❖ What is the congregation doing to prepare members to take on responsibilities in Christian witness, as they follow their own vocations in and beyond the church?
- ❖ What does leading look like?

Established In the established phase, all the dangers that threaten the dynamic phase have come to pass. Change is not valued or sought. As a result, leadership is disappearing and being replaced by loyalty and sacrifice. The fundamental challenge is to recognize that the church is slowly losing its edge.

Cultural complacence usually squashes any attempt to begin the conversation needed to recognize the true state of affairs.

To lead here, pastor and members must be willing to ask themselves deeper questions. It is time to consider whether the congregation truly desires new members to participate and even to suggest new ways to fulfill the vision. It is time to check whether the congregation's organizational structure and administrative practices are becoming ends in themselves. Fundamentally, *a church in the established phase needs to ask itself if its current vision continues to express God's call in this time and in the place where the church finds itself.*

* What signs do you see of self-satisfaction?
* What has happened to the church's vision?
* What has happened to church members who joined three years ago?
* How much of the church's energy is given to the office, building maintenance, budget tweaking, and the like? What does the church board talk about during a typical meeting?
* What do you permit your pastor to initiate? What does the church consider to be leadership?

Weakening In this phase, leadership hardly can be found, if at all. The congregation has been functioning in a "getting-by" mode for some time. The dominant subculture of the congregation has been in charge for a long time. Members, pastors, or staff with energy and new ideas have been tolerated at best. There probably is a story or two being hidden from the public eye about unpleasant squabbles.

Since vision has virtually disappeared early in this phase, church members do not know what leadership looks like. *To attempt to lead, the pastor first must earn the trust and respect* of a membership who is quietly scared and unable to imagine. Adoption creates cultural capital for the pastor, who will need plenty to help the church face its fears. Only then will it be possible to look forward with any hope.

* Of what are the members most afraid?

- Who believes that they have the right to get their way?
- What would it take to begin an honest conversation about your congregation's future?
- What could you do to help your pastor understand you better and earn your trust?

Leading in the Swamp

Based on discussions in previous chapters, we can highlight a few key hints about leading in the swamp. For one thing, *leading begins with an act of courage*—to identify in the church's mud those submerged beliefs that bear upon the congregation's entire life. It takes courage on behalf of the church board to begin such a process, to keep it going, and to wrestle with what is found, to use those discoveries in making decisions, and to face the anxieties of uncertainty. Inevitably, some well-meaning church member will suggest that the work is not necessary or, worse yet, is dangerous. Watch out, for cultural inertia is strong!

For another thing, learning a new model is not easy. To stay on track, the group working through the swamp process needs to make sure that it understands each cultural layer. For instance, the most common mistake is assuming that a "saying" is actually a "submerged belief." Most people need practice to distinguish between the middle and bottom layers and then to name examples. *Staying clear with the model reduces confusion along the way.*

A third point is, *stick with it.* Don't let your chances for new opportunity and vitality fade by abandoning the very processes that will help you. It takes many months, even some years, before your church mud can reflect new direction and energy. Like the Israelites still wandering in the wilderness, your church might feel as though it is getting nowhere. Your pastor and the church team will be leading as they encourage you to stay the course.[3]

Processes for cultural discovery and application are suggested earlier in this book, especially in part 1. Our point here is that courage, clarity, and constancy used in this way signals a movement of collective will that can eventuate in leadership.

Leading with Streams of Culture

Clues to the future of the declining church are to be found in the very environment that is changing around it. If the church has enough will to look at current census information, for instance, it will learn something. Consider also what is happening to all the sets of submerged beliefs that are represented by all of your community's constituents. Submerged beliefs are not easily created. Proposals for new stuff on the shore or new sayings in the water might strike fear into the hearts of longtime church members.

We have discussed already the initial role that honest and respectful conversation plays in any change process. You want a church board that works with your pastor to help the church talk openly about the world around you. After all, your original purpose was to provide ministry where you are. Genuine ministry is always contextual. Learning together takes openness; doing something about it triggers the potential for leadership.

LEADING AS GROWING EDGE

These several cultural insights about leading suggest a few general themes. First, being able to lead first means *being able to learn*. This is as true for the person seeking to lead as it is for a church committee or board. By "learning," we mean the ways that a person or group finds out what it needs to know, in order to address an issue. A colleague of mine tells the story of a church that decided it wanted to provide day care for its neighborhood. The church spent a full year making the preparations. Then, the week that the church's center opened, the county opened a day care center there too. A bit of initial investigation would have led to this discovery and would have helped the church decide about its own plans. Churches need to identify what they do not know that would help them make decisions and meet goals.

Second, being able to lead involves *learning from one's own experiences with marginality.* This term might sound like a reference to something negative. For our purposes, marginality is used in a distinctive way to mean a condition or situation of an individual or group that identifies them in some way as being on a fringe. There are all kinds of ways a person or a group might recognize how it is outside of the norm, unusual, or marginal. A teenage girl might be the only female in the advanced mathematics or science courses at her high school. An adult might have spent childhood dealing with a serious physical or medical condition that limited his or her activities and options. One neighborhood in your town of mostly European Americans might be Hispanic day laborers.

These examples, however, only begin to suggest how complex marginality can be. One person or group can fit into society certain ways and not fit in other ways. Age, gender, race, national origin, education, occupation, income, residential neighborhood—these and other features combine dizzying permutations in today's world. Depending on where I am, what I am doing, or with whom I am engaged, I could feel right at home in one moment and marginal later that day.

Working through the discomfort of one's own marginal status in a constructive way is one of the hallmarks of preparing oneself to be able to lead. *One of the key characteristics that a leader needs is experience with marginality.* This insight applies not only to individual persons, but also—even more—to groups such as congregations. What can your church identify out of its history and/or its present circumstances that give it a marginal quality?

A third way that cultural strategies suggest leadership is in *paying attention to things to which most people don't pay attention.* Becoming aware of every group's own cultural swamp; figuring out the streams of culture in your church's context; talking lifecycle language without feeling threatened by what you discover: learning how to observe is a skill in itself. Gaining helpful skills is a hallmark of leading.

Fourth, *leading results from more than just a call.* Just because you are called does not mean that you are ready. It takes times of observing, trying, failing, reflecting, being supported, and the like to prepare for ministry—whether as a pastor or as a congregation. No wonder, then, that leading itself can be a rare commodity. This book can help your church prepare to be ready to lead.

THE CONGREGATION AS LEADER

One of the ways that a church contributes to leadership is by *fostering the development of its members.* What is it about the life of your congregation that promotes personal growth in faith, resourceful capacities for living, and significant participation in various forms of ministry? If you are not sure, then your church is not leading anyone or anything.

We need to speak also about leadership and *congregational marginality.* Taking the opportunity, every local church can discern some way in which it does not "fit in." Engaging in this exercise will open the doors for a profound, fresh understanding of a church's purpose. One church in Chicago took this step, at a critical juncture in its early life. Founded in the early 1960s by well-educated, middle-class African Americans, this congregation witnessed a dramatic transition in its midst. White flight left the community filled with poverty and despair. The young church struggled to find its place. It had lost two-thirds of its members and was searching for a pastor to help give it direction. It found one.

Fifteen years later, this church had five thousand members, an extensive educational program, local mission with the nearby housing projects, a large youth ministry, more than two dozen of its members in seminary, and a large construction project to triple its physical plant. What happened? Key to its achievement was the way in which their new pastor helped the congregation to frame its ethnic history of racial, social, and economic marginality in fresh ways. It had discovered how to affirm, together as a community of faith, a way of living from the edge.

Unfortunately, not many congregations face their marginality in this way. What is often missing in such churches is a capacity for engaging biblical narrative in the context of community. As the scriptural witness indicates in many places, *the people of God are called to remember the stories of their past, their struggles, and the acts of God on their behalf* (see, for instance, Joshua 24). Much of what constitutes such stories can be interpreted as living in and through marginality.

Coming to terms with one's distinctive experiences with marginality is one example of learning how to learn together.

Church-wide conversations should include inquiries among members about what the church needs to discover. This means learning how to see, to think together, to understand more deeply than one perfunctory monthly meeting allows. By taking on the tasks of discovery, your church comes to realize that learning is an integral part of the rhythm of church vitality. *A vital congregation adopts a posture of humility.* In a world of rapidly occurring change, organizations who are content with their view of things have lost the perspective they need to stay in the game.

Organizational learning and humility lead us back again to the cultural framework for this book. To lead means to help discern, clarify, and follow a fresh vision. By so doing, a church eventually attains, sustains, or regains the dynamic qualities that serve it best. Thus leadership pursues this very specific purpose. Anything else is either managing or administering, both of which are necessary responsibilities. However, neither one can create vision; that is the task of leading.

PAYOFF TIME: CREATING SHARED LEADERSHIP[4]

Our discussion of leadership in this chapter so far has given limited attention to the pastor. This omission has been intentional. All too often, organizations behave as though the only ones who can lead are those "at the top." After all, is that not why they are there? Persons in top offices do not always lead. *Leadership does not always emerge in the obvious places.* Jesus himself was not regarded by the religious or political officials of his day as anyone worthy to follow. By keeping the spotlight off of your pastor, perhaps you will see more readily that leadership is something to be shared.

What would this look like for your church and its pastor? As we conclude this book, itself being an exploration into new ways of thinking, let us draw together more of the major points that have emerged. These points summarize much of the practical focus of this book, offering you a glimpse into the qualities that make leading a partnership.

Trusting, Talking, and Telling

Perhaps there is no other way to lay the groundwork for leading than to develop a strong sense of *respect, trust, and capacity for dialogue.* The significance of this quality has garnered attention outside of religion, in recent discussions about effective business management[5] and of international economic success.[6] In order for leadership to develop in a community, people need to hold each other in esteem, valuing each other's presence and contributions. As we have seen, this kind of relationship develops between your church and its pastor, as an "adoption" process (chapter 4). Out of respectful, probing conversations, your pastor, your church board, and your key culture bearers create both a bond and the beginnings of direction.

As trust and respect develop, the next step is coming to terms with the condition of the congregation as it is. In most cases, this aspect of leadership has to do with the difficult business of truth-naming. *Our churches cannot become all that God aims for them without a healthy dose of spiritual honesty.*

What streams of culture in your community are new or changing? Which elements of the stuff on your church's cultural shore are connected to which submerged beliefs in the mud? Which can foster fresh vision and which submerged beliefs will get in the way? Questions like these, pursued together thoughtfully, set the stage for leading.

Follow the Stars

At the center of leading is vision. How can your church work with your pastor to *discern a fresh version of its vision?* Vision is a set of sayings discerned in some relationship to each other, which the congregation comes to accept as its call from God into the future. Many of these vision sayings could be familiar. What gives vision its edge and motivation, however, are those newer sayings, emerging out of new insights about your community. *The strongest visions are born in the struggle of a group to discern together on behalf of the congregation.* You want your pastor to be one of the key persons in this process.

Once a vision has been embraced, the work begins. Leadership is not detail work alone! But leadership cannot be exercised without *attention to detail*. Many decisions will need to be made, along a broad scale of issues. You can expect to deal with misunderstandings, unexpected events, member resistance, and more. Keep reminding everyone that, in order to stay faithful to the gospel, the church has to keep learning. *Only learners can become leaders.*

Along the way, vision gets tested. To lead during testing is to feel like Moses in the wilderness, like Jeremiah buying property as Jerusalem falls, or like Jesus at his ascension. A faith community struggling with its future would rather be back in Egypt than face the deserts of uncertainty. To lead in such a time is to apply elements of the vision judiciously. In one way or another, every church finding its way again needs to affirm what it knows of God. You will want your pastor to offer this guidance, not glibly, but out of a deep sense of the workings of God in the world.

Perhaps the final thing to say about sharing leadership with your pastor is that it takes *patience*. Any enterprise that is worth its salt needs to be led, and that takes time. How can you behave in such a way that anxious or skeptical members see your deep belief that the Holy Spirit is working in your midst? Beyond what anyone can see at any moment, beyond what you know for sure, beyond even what we can imagine, stands a God who never sleeps. *To lead is to use all of our wisdom and skill toward a faithful vision, and then let God be at work.* The congregation needs to see your pastor and your church officers lead in this way.

Leadership is not a commodity that can be bought or exchanged like a loaf of bread or an expensive automobile. To some extent, we cannot know if "leading" has occurred until after the fact, when we see what eventually has transpired. In this regard, leadership is spiritual, almost evasive, like the wind in the fourth Gospel that blows where it chooses (John 3:8). Yet we cannot do without it, or our communities and churches suffer. Your partnership with your church's pastor can make all the difference to leadership. You just might end up surprised at what God can do through you, when you learn how to get along with your pastor.

❖

RESOURCE LIST

For more information about the theoretical foundations and the practical applications found in this book, the following books are recommended:

Adizes, Ichak. *Corporate Lifecycles: How and Why Corporations Grow and Die and What to Do about It*. Englewood Cliffs, N.J.: Prentice Hall, 1988.

_____. *Managing Corporate Lifecycles*. Paramus, N.J.: Prentice Hall, 1999.

Schein, Edgar. *Organizational Culture and Leadership*, 2nd ed. San Francisco: Jossey-Bass, 1992.

_____. *The Corporate Culture Survival Guide*. San Francisco: Jossey-Bass, 1999.

Thompson, George B., Jr., ed. *Alligators in the Swamp: Power, Ministry, and Leadership*. Cleveland: Pilgrim Press, 2005.

_____. *Futuring Your Church: Finding Your Vision and Making It Work*. Cleveland: United Church Press, 1999.

_____. *How to Get Along with Your Church: Creating Cultural Capital for Doing Ministry*. Cleveland: Pilgrim Press, 2001.

_____. *Treasures in Clay Jars: New Ways to Understand Your Church*. Cleveland: Pilgrim Press, 2003.

❖

NOTES

Introduction

1. See, for instance, Speed Leas and Paul Kittlaus, *Church Fights* (Philadelphia: Westminster Press, 1973); Speed Leas, *Leadership and Conflict* (Nashville: Abingdon Press, 1982); Hugh Halverstedt, *Managing Church Conflict* (Louisville: Westminster John Knox Press, 1991); and Charles H. Cosgrove and Dennis D. Hatfield, *Church Conflict: The Hidden Systems behind the Fights* (Nashville: Abingdon Press, 1994).

2. Edwin H. Friedman, *Generation to Generation: Family Process in Church and Synagogue* (New York and London: Guilford, 1985).

Chapter 1

1. The following descriptive images of churches come from Carl S. Dudley and Sally A. Johnson, *Energizing the Congregation: Images that Shape Your Church's Ministry* (Louisville: Westminster John Knox Press, 1993). They are summarized on pages 6–7 and then elaborated upon in respective book chapters.

2. These categories (reality, truth, time, space, human nature, and human relationships) are described in detail in Edgar Schein, *Organizational Culture and Leadership,* 2nd ed. (San Francisco: Jossey-Bass, 1992), chapters 6, 7.

3. For concise summaries of the use of the Greek terms *chronos* and *kairos,* see Walter Bauer, William F. Arndt, and F.

Wilbur Gingrich, *A Greek-English Lexicon of the New Testament and Other Early Christian Literature,* 2nd ed. revised by F. Wilbur Gingrich and Frederick W. Danker (Chicago and London: University of Chicago Press, 1979), 394–95 (*kairos*) and 887–88 (*chronos*).

Chapter 2

1. Literature in organizational theory is extensive. Some of the notable titles over the years include James G. March and Herbert A. Simon, with the collaboration of Harold Guetzkow, *Organizations* (New York: John Wiley & Sons, 1958); W. Richard Scott, *Organizations: Rational, Natural, and Open Systems,* 4th ed. (Upper Saddle River, N.J.: Prentice-Hall, 1998); Charles Perrow, *Complex Organizations: A Critical Essay,* 3rd ed. (New York: McGraw-Hill, 1986); and Lee G. Bolman and Terrence E. Deal, *Reframing Organizations: Artistry, Choice, and Leadership,* 3rd ed. (San Francisco: Jossey-Bass, 2003).

2. Ichak Adizes writes in one of his later books about the central role that "relate" (he calls it "integrate" or "include") can play in an organization's strength and resiliency throughout the lifecycle, especially in the early phase. See Adizes, *Managing Corporate Lifecycles* (Paramus, N.J.: Prentice Hall Press, 1999), chapter 18, "The Optimal Path;" see also page 401, point IV.

3. Edgar Schein's discussion concerning submerged beliefs ("basic shared assumptions") about time are very pertinent here. A learning culture, he says, is oriented to time as between "near-future" and "far-future" (*Organizational Culture and Leadership,* 2nd ed. (San Francisco: Jossey-Bass, 1992), 369). This focus of time, and the organization's willingness to learn, are characteristics of what we are calling here the dynamic phase.

Chapter 3

1. Treatment of the notion of social class is extensive in sociological literature. My own thinking on this subject has been influenced by Max Weber; see his "Class, Status Groups, and Parties," in *Weber: Selections in Translation,* ed. W. G. Runciman, trans.

Eric Matthews (Cambridge: Cambridge University Press, 1978), 43–56.

2. Tex Sample, *Ministry in an Oral Culture: Living with Will Rogers, Uncle Remus, and Minnie Pearl* (Louisville: Westminster John Knox Press, 1994).

3. A helpful sociological study of white ethnic groups in the United States is Andrew M. Greeley's *Why Can't They Be Like Us? America's White Ethnic Groups* (New York: E.P. Dutton, 1971).

4. See Jean Bethke Elshtain, *Jane Addams and the Dream of American Democracy: A Life* (New York: Basic Books, 2002).

5. For a generational theory developed by a theologian for use by churches, see Douglas Walrath, *Frameworks: Patterns for Living and Believing Today* (Cleveland: Pilgrim Press, 1987). For an elaborate theory of generations that analyzes American history, see William Strauss and Neil Howe, *Generations: The History of America's Future, 1584–2069* (New York: William Morrow, 1991). Walrath's theory, while not as extensive in historical scope or conceptual depth, is consistent with Strauss and Howe's.

6. George B. Thompson Jr., *How to Get Along with Your Church: Creating Cultural Capital for Doing Ministry* (Cleveland: Pilgrim Press, 2001), 38.

Chapter 4

1. A three-stage process for becoming "assimilated" into a new community is described by Anthony J. Gittins, which I have adapted and used in *How to Get Along with Your Church* (Cleveland: Pilgrim Press, 2001), 30–33. See Gittins' book *Gifts and Strangers: Meeting the Challenge of Inculturation* (New York: Paulist Press, 1989), chapter 5. The description that follows in this chapter draws from Gittins.

2. See Edgar Schein, *Organizational Culture and Leadership*, 3rd ed. (San Francisco: Jossey-Bass, 1992), chapter 13, for more details of this "embedding" process.

3. For a creative interpretation of the Day of Pentecost story (Acts 2) as an experience of both speaking and of hearing, see

Eric Law, *The Wolf Shall Dwell with the Lamb* (St. Louis: Chalice Press, 1993), chapter 5.

Chapter 5

1. This figure is based on a count of the number of "power" entries in *Nelson's Complete Concordance of the Revised Standard Version Bible* (New York: Thomas Nelson & Sons, 1957), 1505–07.

2. Change processes are described in Edgar Schein, *The Corporate Culture Survival Guide* (San Francisco: Jossey-Bass, 1999), chapter six, and in John P. Kotter, *Leading Change* (Boston: Harvard Business School Press, 1996). Kotter's process begins with "establishing a sense of urgency" and moves secondly to "creating a guiding coalition"; see Kotter, chapters 3 and 4.

Chapter 6

1. The names of some of these persons and groups are Speed Leas, Lloyd Rediger, Hugh Halverstad, Peter Steinke, Lombard Mennonite Peace Center, Bridge Builders (London), and the Alban Institute.

2. This saying, well-known among African American congregations, has an organizational parallel in Edgar Schein, *Organizational Culture and Leadership* (San Francisco: Jossey-Bass, 1992), 371–72. Schein writes of organizations needing to recognize that the world is not simple and that solutions emerge when the organization learns to become "a perpetual learning system."

3. Schein speaks of group learning requiring submerged beliefs about the world around it being "to some degree manageable" and about human beings as "proactive problem solvers," in *Organizational Culture and Leadership*, 364.

Chapter 7

1. Robert K. Greenleaf, *Servant Leadership: A Journey into the Nature of Legitimate Power and Greatness* (New York: Paulist Press, 1977), 61–65.

2. Readers who are curious to find out more about leadership theory can peruse such authors, besides Edgar Schein and Robert

Greenleaf, as Warren Bennis, *On Becoming a Leader* (New York: Addison-Wesley, 1989); John Gardner, *On Leadership* (New York: Free Press, 1990); Margaret Wheatley, *Leadership and the New Science* (San Francisco: Berrett-Koehler, 1992); Ronald Heifitz, *Leadership without Easy Answers* (Cambridge: Harvard University Press, 1994); James M. Kouzes and Barry Z. Pozner, *The Leadership Challenge* (San Francisco: Jossey-Bass, 1987); Daniel Goleman, Richard Boyatzis, and Annie McKee, *Primal Leadership* (Boston: Harvard Business School Press, 2002); and John Kotter, *Leading Change* (Boston: Harvard Business School Press, 1996). Some readers might be interested to look at articles in the *Journal of Religious Leadership*, found on the website www.christianleaders.org.

3. John Kotter's sixth step for leading organizational change is to target and fulfill a few short-term accomplishments. These have the effect of demonstrating to the group members that change is possible, is desirable, and gives everyone a boost of confidence. See his *Leading Change* (Cambridge: Harvard Business School Press, 1997), 21 and chapter 8.

4. For readers who would like a sound introductory presentation on church leadership, I recommend Lovett Weems' book *Church Leadership: Vision, Team, Culture, and Integrity* (Nashville: Abingdon Press, 1993).

5. See Ichak Adizes, *Mastering Change: The Power of Mutual Trust and Respect* (Santa Monica, Calif.: Adizes Publications, 1992), especially conversation 10.

6. See Francis Fukuyama, *Trust: The Social Virtues and the Creation of Prosperity* (New York: Free Press, 1995).